DROPSHIPPING
RICHE$

JUMPSTART YOUR SHOPIFY STORE
THIS WEEKEND TO $10,000/MO.

Without AliExpress, Amazon, or Facebook Ads -
Proven System Using Dropshipping and Print on
Demand Strategies for Explosive Growth

KAT OLSEN

Paperback: 978-1-959951-00-1
Caselaminate: 978-1-959951-01-8
Kindle: 978-1-959951-02-5
ACX Audio: 978-1-959951-03-2

Table of Contents

About the Author

Kat Olsen is not new to the business world. She has over 25 years of experience in business startups. More specifically, she has experience in internet business building, marketing, and training. What's more, she has been a mentor to thousands over the years. She has worked in Digital Marketing Management roles for some of the largest media and digital marketing agencies in the world.

To add to this already impressive resume, Kat has personally developed, launched, and grown over 11 successful Shopify dropshipping e-commerce businesses over the past 6 years. She has worked in dropshipping, print-on-demand, design, Etsy, marketing, and wholesale. Kat has also been a certified Shopify Developer partner for the past 5 years.

In working through other training programs, failing miserably and succeeding wildly, testing her hypotheses and methods, she shares what does and does not work. She has had explosive growth into and beyond the $10K/month benchmark. She has coached Olympic Gold

Medalists, best-selling authors such as Cynthia Daddona, successful CEOs, construction workers, nurses, website designers, university marketing directors, internet business gurus, authors, infopreneurs, real estate investors and agents, restaurant owners, graphic artists, eBay merchants, event planners, network marketers, home-based businesses, stay-at-home moms and even other successful coaches in how to build and scale your business online.

This book is not a sales tool for an overpriced coaching or training program.

This book contains Kat's specific journey to $10k+/month, showing everything she has done to succeed and helping you avoid the painful and expensive common pitfalls and get to your $10k profits faster.

Introduction

"Dropshipping is a great business model that gives you an opportunity to work online and be your own boss."

— JENNIFER TOMPSON

There is a lot of information available to help you grow your dropshipping business. So much so that it can be overwhelming. For this reason, this book has been skillfully organized to help you to understand everything you need to know in the clearest way possible. As such the book is divided into nine chapters.

Chapter 1- Dropshipping Today

◆ The first chapter will act as a sort of extension of this introduction. It will discuss the trends of dropshipping and why it has become so popular as a method of business.

Chapter 2- The Reasons You're Not Earning

◆ This second chapter will tackle the truths that perhaps may be difficult to accept. We will take a hard look into perhaps why your business isn't as successful as it could be.

Chapter 3- Choosing A Trending Niche

◆ Here we will explore the trends of dropshipping and how you can choose the right niche for you.

Chapter 4- Work With the Best Suppliers

◆ Unless you can make everything yourself you will have to work with suppliers. This fourth chapter will help you navigate those relationships.

Chapter 5- Create a Professional Store, Redesigning Your Website

◆ The first impressions are important but difficult to make when your business is online. This is why you should learn how to design your website to make that perfect impression for you.

Chapter 6- Features and Integrations

◆ Of course, having a good first impression is only one step. You also need to have inviting features and ways for your customers to interact with your site.

Chapter 7- High Ticket Dropshipping and Print On Demand

◆ Most dropshippers focus solely on low-end products often out of fear of delving into dropshipping more expensive items or high ticket goods. Contrary to what such entrepreneurs may think, high ticket dropshipping is a highly lucrative niche. You can even print most of such items on demand very easily! We will discuss all these in great detail in this chapter.

Chapter 8- Customer Service

◆ It can be easy to forget that your customers are people since your business will largely operate online. For this reason, we have purposely set aside a chapter to discuss the different ways to maintain excellent customer service.

Chapter 9- Building Brand Awareness

◆ The last chapter in the book is reserved for your brand and making sure your brand is working for you.

Essentially, this book will give you everything you need to know to have a thriving dropshipping business.

1.

Dropshipping Today

Did you know that the dropshipping industry is undergoing one of its most explosive growth spurts yet? It's true, and since you are already operating with this business model, this means that you are on track to get good returns on your investments. For some context, this business model was recently assessed at 162.44 billion dollars back in 2019 (Business Wire, 2020). Impressive, right? Well, today the market for dropshipping is anticipated to rise at a CAGR of 18.3% from 2019 to 2027 when it is predicted to be profitable enough to return some US$ 591.77 billion annually (Business Wire, 2020).

Customer gadgets like tablets, cell phones, as well as laptops are becoming more and more popular in developing economies, which opens up the new and exciting potential for numerous continuing advancements in technology. These devices are now more widely used in both developing and developed economies. The customer electronics sector alone in developing nations has a ton of room to grow, and consumption is expected to soar as brand penetration rises. In the coming years, it's anticipated that demand for customer electronics like televisions and refrigerators will rise.

Why does this business model resonate with modern-day entrepreneurs like you and me? The answer to this is simple. Well, we both know that we live in an age where most people, particularly millennials, quickly adopt new buying fads. Online shopping is all the rave and customers across the globe are quite addicted to the convenience of shopping on their smartphones.

These trends make it easy for entrepreneurs and business owners to advertise daily, take orders quickly and direct the delivery of the items bought from your suppliers straight to the customers. All while making some good profit!

Dropshipping is a business model where everyone benefits. On one hand, the manufacturer need not worry about all the expenses associated with branding, marketing, or developing a market niche for their goods. In fact, they will have such a backlog of orders that the only expenditures they would be concerned about are ones related to the production and delivery of their goods to retailers or dropshippers and their customers.

The retailer, on the other hand, is only concerned with marketing and listing the products that they deem appropriate for sale on the website. There are no overhead expenditures, fees associated with the storage of products, or having to sell surplus items for a discount. Retailers have no control over the manufacturing process and may not even see the products as these are shipped off directly to the customers by the supplier.

A smart retailer should, however, keep track of products sold under his/her name because customers only interact with their brand and are typically unaware of the supplier behind the scenes. This means that in the event of defective goods or shipping delays, the dropshipper often assumes complete liability. This is just a part of doing business.

The Dropshipping Market Size

Despite its minimal start-up expenses and inventory-free setup, dropshipping has grown to be one of the most well-liked internet business models in recent years. In fact, the most recent research on this indicates that the global dropshipping industry will have grown by a staggering 23.7% from 2021 to 2022, reaching $196.78 billion (Oberlo, 2022). Many familiar websites you may know about are dropshippers like Wayfair.com, Overstock.com, Bluecrate.com, TrendyGoods, and more.

Not only that but it is anticipated that this amount will keep growing in the years to come, topping $200 billion for the first time in 2023 and landing somewhere in the $243.42 billion range (Oberlo, 2022). These findings indicate a persistent and quick rise. The market for dropshipping is expected to increase even further, reaching $301.11 billion in 2024, $372.47 billion in 2025 and eventually up to $476.1 billion by 2026. To put things in perspective, this represents a growth of $347.5 billion in just six years (Oberlo, 2022)!

As you can imagine, this huge expansion of the dropshipping market has been aided in no small measure by the growth of online shopping all over the world. You can have a piece of that pie.

During the Coronavirus outbreak of 2020, millions of people were forced to stay at home as most physical stores closed down operations for months, if not years, some permanently. People were forced to use the internet as their only shopping option due to these restrictions, and as a result, the global eCommerce industry rose exponentially.

Aside from the foregoing though, dropshipping's expanding market size is also a result of how simple it is to get started. Owners of businesses do not need to keep inventory, therefore there is no need for storage space and no upfront expenditure for purchasing merchandise. All of these mean that the start-up costs of a dropshipping business are significantly less than that of a traditional business model. Who wouldn't be drawn to that?! Make no mistake, there are still costs involved, but it's a very low barrier to entry.

Is It Still Profitable?

If you're struggling to make a profit in your dropshipping business, I completely understand. That was my business the first 2 years as I learned about better US-based suppliers and better Shopify themes, better marketing. From experience, I can tell you that the key to your success as a dropshipper is selecting the best products, keeping your profit margins high enough, and partnering with suppliers that have true wholesale prices and fast shipping, that you can trust. That's it! You can grow a successful, lucrative online dropshipping business if you cover those bases.

The truth is that many of you are growing your dropshipping business from the comfort of your home today, provided you build your eCommerce website, locate credible suppliers, and choose products you can start with and test. Then, with time, consistency, and patience, you can watch as the money starts to come in.

Why is Dropshipping so Popular?

Today, the dropshipping market is valued at $197 billion, up 53% from 2020, and experts estimate the market to be about five hundred billion dollars by the year 2027 (Globe News Wire, 2020). As previously mentioned, the popularity of dropshipping today was greatly influenced by the COVID-19 pandemic because many people shopped online more frequently than they did before the pandemic. Apart from this though, dropshipping also got very popular because of certain advantages. Let us discuss a few of these briefly below.

The Benefits of Dropshipping

Low Entrance Threshold

Regardless of whether or not you are just starting out, dropshipping is an awesome way for you to make money today. You don't need to spend tons of cash, stocking up on products as a dropshipper. All you have to do is advertise to your target audience, secure their orders, remit some of their payments to your supplier, and keep your profits.

Flexibility

You can use your business to provide as many goods as you like. If you have a 9-5 day job, you won't have to quit or reduce your hours to fit in time for your dropshipping business. You can start it as a side hustle while enjoying the security of your monthly salary. You can also work from wherever you want as the business model here is a highly flexible one.

Ease of Accessibility and Tests

As a retailer or dropshipper, your primary focus should be assessing the kind of products that sell quickly. Refining this process will come with time and testing. This is because other responsibilities —like product delivery and shipping—have been removed from your plate. For this reason, your focus can remain on marketing.

Is Dropshipping Profitable?

Yes, but most times there is a cap on the amount of profit you can make on every item you sell, especially as dropshippers frequently pay slightly higher prices to get products from suppliers. The convenience of avoiding manufacturing, and shipment issues come at a price, one that isn't too high to bear.

The truth is that almost any dropshipping business can be successful given the correct conditions. It all depends on what you sell and how heavily you are investing in advertising strategies. If you choose the proper items to sell at the appropriate price, it is possible.

Dropshipping can become an expensive business model, particularly when you incorporate advertising, (video, email marketing, social media marketing, etc). However, recovering your capital can be done easily and the business can generate its own cash flow in a matter of weeks or months.You can also access very reasonable and REAL wholesale prices from certain resources that we will go over later in the book.

How Competitive is Dropshipping?

Dropshipping is a powerful business strategy for entrepreneurs wishing to sell things online because anyone can get started with it for free. As a result, this business model is quite competitive, especially if you sell in a well-known dropshipping market such as clothing, home improvement products, and accessories like jewelry or handbags. Fortunately, you can set yourself apart from the competition by doing the following things:

Choosing a Market that's Less Congested

Any new dropshipping niche is assessed based on the following factors: The number of searches per day (over 100), the degree of competition (who ranks on page 1), and the likelihood that the products are available in a broad selection of local shops, as well as the average retail price of $100 at minimum. If there are a good number of brands already selling your flagship product, continue to research and try selling some other product.

Also, consider "niching" down within an already existing market. This means that if your target audience is too broad, such as "pet owners," you may niche down to "dog owners" or "cat owners." If you find the market still too saturated, you may consider niching down further to a specific dog breed such as "pug owners."

This does not limit your ability to make money, it is actually an effective tactic to bring in more money.

Putting Customer Service First

The most unsuccessful dropshippers I know make the mistake of concentrating entirely on marketing while ignoring their existing customers. Don't do this. Your current customers are your most loyal customers, precisely because they are more likely to buy the things you're offering than your future customers. While advertising to new target customers, ensure that your existing customers are so happy with their experience so that they keep coming back for more. This could be through creating loyalty programs and affiliate/ambassador programs.

Establishing a Credible Brand

I have amassed a great deal of money and experience from my drop-shipping businesses over the years and I can tell you that a smart way to succeed in dropshipping today is to cultivate your business identity both as a brand and an authentic, legitimate company. It is really important to cultivate the faith of your customers in your brand. They must think of you as credible and reliable; otherwise, the products you advertise may not see the light of day.

Even when you secure your first customers, always remember that there is room for improvement. Be vigilant of ways to make customers trust your brand more and more. Think of how to make their user experience better, where to source higher-quality products, or how to ship their order quicker than before.

How Long Does it Take to Succeed?

As the saying goes, nothing good comes easy. Even though dropship-ping is a low-risk business model, you still need to put in the work before you can succeed in it. Starting an online business, sourcing new products, assessing suppliers, marketing your products, and developing a brand are all included in this. There is no definitive answer to how long it takes to succeed. I got my first sale from my first website within 9 days of launch. That doesn't mean you should expect that, but my point is, this is possible.

In practical terms, for your dropshipping business to make up to $2,000 per month in sales, plan on working at least 10 to 15 hours per week. When you break that down, it's really only 2-3 hours a day. This is because, just like any other venture, investing more time into your business increases your chances of making more profit and succeeding more quickly.

New Trends in Dropshipping

Dropshipping has a very promising future. When refining your niche, take your time and allow it to evolve as you continue to research products and target audiences. It may be clothing, accessories, cuisine, books, home furnishings, or jewelry. Make sure to carefully choose your audience if you want to stand out. You need to know who your target audience is and what kinds of products you are selling to them at all times.

The trick is to get into the target audience's head and engage in the dialogue going on in their head when they land on your website or the product page. Engage that dialogue within the first 5-10 seconds and your chances of a sale increase exponentially.

Sell a lot of different unrelated items all at once and you risk confusing your potential customers, so always pay attention to what your customers are thinking and saying. Make a plan to market the products that your audience is drawn to and that they relate to. Imagine that people associate your name with a passion they want to pursue, an activity they like, or a way of life improvement. If so, such customers will stick with you even if you enter a new market.

Establish trust by providing high-quality goods on schedule and retrieving customer complaints timely. Your customers must be able to develop trust in your judgment. Create a brand name for your business that stands out and draws in more customers gradually because this can take time.

A number of dropshipping trends are generating headlines for 2022. They consist of the following.

Optimizing on Mobile Devices

With the increased use of mobile phones, business revenues increase because viewers start to rely more on the responsive interface of business apps. Mobile phones are simple to use, accessible, and convenient for shopping. Since mobile payments are safe and dependable, the majority of customers today choose their purchases on their smartphones and are even prepared to pay on the spot. Make sure your website is compatible with both mobile devices and desktop computers.

In addition, ensure your listings are optimized for mobile. With certain shopping ads, your listings page is your landing page. Most of your visitors do not land on your home page.

Private Messaging and Chatbots

You'd be amazed to learn how many customers want websites to contact them through chatbots and artificial intelligence. Chatbots are efficient means of responding to complaints, clarifying complicated processes, and answering commonly asked questions from customers, in real-time as they are shopping on your website. Additionally, chatbots gather user data, search needs, and patterns to produce tailored search results. Don't be afraid to use them. Some popular ones for Shopify are Messenger and Shopify Inbox.

Personalization

As a dropshipper, offering personalized products or solutions to your customers is a great way to keep them coming back to your website. Something as simple as a personalized mug, sticker, journal, hand-written note, or another little gift will make your customers feel appreciated and secure their loyalty to your brand. Such personal touches are also relatively easy to incorporate and add a personal feel to your dropshipping services.

This is also where the practice of "Print on Demand" comes in. This is a business model where you direct your supplier to make products to be sold under your brand name using your unique designs. Put differently, you collaborate with your printer/supplier to customize the products you wish to sell. You don't pay for the item until after you've sold it, just like the standard dropshipping model. As such, you would have no need to keep any inventory or make major purchases.

Print-on-demand is a more hands-on approach to the product's look than the dropshipping business model, even though both models deal with purchasing products from reliable suppliers that package and ship them to the customers. Also, since there is a higher level of involvement in the print-on-demand model, there is often more delay due to production times of the customized products than what is tenable under the dropshipping business model.

Regardless of these differences, my point here is simple: if you do a good job and show your personal appreciation for the customer, they are more likely to refer you. We will go more into print-on-demand in a later chapter.

Simple Checkouts

Did you know that 2 out of 3 customers abandon their shopping carts on business websites daily? It's true! Oftentimes this happens because the checkout process has become too cumbersome for them due to last-minute hidden fees or there being too many clicks before the payment is complete.

If you want your customers to complete payment on your site after shopping, you must ensure that the check-out process is as seamless as possible for them. Introduce several payment options as well as security measures to protect your customer's information. When using Shopify payments, you automatically accept all the major credit cards plus some.

In addition, you could sign up for an Amazon Pay account, PayPal and Shop Pay to offer more flexible models of payment for your customer.

Key Takeaways

In this chapter we addressed going back over the basics of dropship-ping. We did this as briefly as possible because you already have an understanding of the dropshipping business model before you picked up this book. Let's look at some of the more important points again here as a summary.

◆ Dropshipping is a kind of business practice in which a seller lists products for sale while they are still with the suppliers rather than maintaining an inventory or warehouse full of goods.

◆ The keys to being a successful dropshipper include selecting great products that are of interest to a target audience,
keeping your profit margins high enough, and partnering with
suppliers you can trust.

◆ Dropshipping is competitive and can become an expensive
business model, particularly when you incorporate advertising, (video, email marketing, social media marketing, google
shopping, etc). However, you can recover your capital when
you embrace new trends, especially in relation to your chosen
niche.

Of course, even though dropshipping can be incredibly popular, some
still aren't making a profit from their stores. In the next chapter, we
will explore some of the reasons why this could be happening.

2.

The Reasons You're Not Earning

I magine that you love jogging with your dog but find it difficult to retain your hold on the leash. A dropshipper might purchase a hands-free jogging leash from eBay or amazon and sell it to you via Instagram. They'll make a video highlighting its advantages, and then pester you with it until you finally cave in and buy the product. But what if, despite all their efforts, you decide not to buy that product? Could such a choice have any justifications? Let's get into more depth about that below.

Reasons Why You May Not Be Making Sales

You can succeed at dropshipping with the appropriate degree of research, hard work, and consistency. However, sometime, new dropshippers fail at making sales and eventually fold up shop. Some of the reasons for this failure include the following.

Poor Collaboration with the Manufacturer

Since every aspect of your business depends on the other party completing their part, collaborating with an unreliable manufacturer would deal a very devastating blow to the integrity of your brand and so, is a recipe for your business failure.

Margin Dissatisfaction

A rule of thumb in the dropshipping business is to aim for a profit margin of between 30% and 40% after all other factors have been balanced. Otherwise, you just might find that your margins are too tight. And when this occurs, many new dropshippers simply quit the business. Do not make the mistake of trying to compete on price alone, however. Loyal customers do not shop on price alone. I go more into that later.

Terrible Track Record with Customers

Customers often only get in touch with you when there is an issue, and they expect you to fix it. When dropshipping, you are the one they get in touch with. The more you deal with such issues poorly, the more customers you would lose.

These are not the only reasons why new dropshippers struggle with turning a profit. Some other reasons for this include the following.

Using Poor Images and Product Descriptions

Customers who shop on your website cannot physically examine the products they like before paying for them. This means that your customers rely on the images and product descriptions you provide on your website. If your product descriptions are difficult to read or if the item photographs are subpar, your business will suffer.

Insufficient Contact Details

You may not realize this but as a dropshipper, presenting limited contact information on your website raises serious concerns in the eyes of customers. They want to know that if there is a problem, they can get in touch with you directly. Even if you do everything else right, you'll struggle to win over customers if you don't display your address (even if you don't have a physical store) and phone number.

You don't have to use your home address, it is recommended for you to get a business address at your local UPS store (theupsstore.com) or online at ipostal1.com, which provide an address similar to having a suite number. Be sure to not just get a PO Box, this doesn't work nearly as well. You can rent a physical business address for as little as $5-10/mo., on average, depending on your location.

You can get a virtual phone number, as well. If you have a mobile phone, you can get a free number at Google Voice. These numbers have to attach to a regular phone, whether it be your mobile or land line. If that's not possible, you can get a paid number at several websites such and MightyCall.com (my favorite) at a very low cost.

Cumbersome Checkout Process

Long and difficult checkout processes are so frustrating to customers that they frequently abandon the products in their cart and quit your website. Keep the check-out process as simple as you can to reduce irritation.

Likewise, never require registration in order to check out. Let your customers follow the steps and decide whether to sign up or save their details for a future visit when they are finished.

Hidden Costs Associated with Shipping
This is one of the key reasons that shoppers ditch their shopping carts across eCommerce platforms today. Fortunately, the answer to this is as easy as including the cost of shipping into your product price and providing free shipping.

A Poorly-Designed Navigation Menu

Did you know that up to 80 percent of buyers use their cell phones to conduct online searches? (SmartInsights, 2022). Before you launch, ensure that your site design is mobile-friendly, that the images are big enough to see on mobile screens, and that your widgets are the right size. Google advises using buttons and tap targets that are at least 48 pixels in height and width. Most Shopify themes work well with this guideline.

Customers are Clueless as to What to Do

You must be extremely clear about what you want the customer to do on your website, even if it is an eCommerce one, or you risk losing them. Never leave your customers confused about what to do next; always provide them with clear instructions. This includes what we call "calls to action." An example would be "Click Now to Buy" or "Buy Now."

Ineffective Marketing

Your store won't make any money if there isn't focused traffic. So as a dropshipper, there is a need to come up with a marketing plan that incorporates paid marketing and social media marketing.

Then, once you start gaining customers, integrate user testimonials and reviews into your marketing plan to increase your social proof and advertise your store. With time, you can even toss in a referral program using technologies like BON Loyalty and Rewards program Shopify app.

Lack of Customer Engagement

For salespeople, the idea of not engaging fully with potential customers is just as detrimental as being too pushy or forceful with ads. Engaging your audience across as many social media platforms as possible is a great way to keep your brand in the spotlight.

But remember, go where your target audience already is which means you can opt to skip some social platforms if you know your audience is not there. For example, if your target audience is 20-25 years old, TikTok may be your best social platform. However, if your audience is 50+, then your best social platform may be Facebook (Meta).

You're Aiming for the Incorrect Demographic

Make sure you conduct detailed audience research so that you know the proper demographic and psychographic you should target in your marketing. Otherwise, you would spend time and money on content marketing with no noticeable returns on your investment.

Issues with Pricing

Putting a price on your products is one of the most challenging aspects of doing business. Set the price too low and people assume that your goods are of poorer quality and may be too suspicious to buy. Set it too high and they run off to buy the same products at lower prices elsewhere.

The process becomes even more difficult when you take tax and shipping charges into account. Finding the pricing sweet spot you need to attract (and keep) customers can only be done after proper market research. You may start by visiting your competition's websites. For the most part, though, you would have to learn this by testing.

The Importance of Website Traffic

Increased internet traffic can help you grow your company, add more products to your range, and create new products. To fully optimize this, read on.

Website Conversions Numbers

The more you can convert your web visitors to paying customers, the quicker you can achieve your business and financial goals. Getting visitors to act in specific ways, whether it's purchasing your product, or subscribing to your email is referred to as "converting" them. It is infinitely better to focus on the website visitors who are interested and ultimately make a purchase than it is to merely count the total number of visits.

Target Market

Your ability to draw in and retain your target audience is crucial to both growing the quantity and quality of website traffic visits to your site. But to do this successfully, you have to know the precise demographic you are marketing your products to, at all times.

Increasing Traffic on your Website

Put more emphasis on benefits than features to drive more traffic to your website. Inform potential customers of the advantages your goods or services will bring them. Instead of concentrating too much on how amazing you and your business are, think about why customers should care about your business and the products they are considering buying.

Repeat Customers

Customers often prefer to remain in their comfort zones and shop from brands they have patronized before. So take the time to remind your loyal customers of the reasons they love buying from you (eg. free shipping, fast delivery, etc). All these are factors that will help your business succeed.

Now as with all other industries, there are a few golden rules of the trade when it comes to the dropshipping business. Let us review these briefly below.

Dropshipping Dos and Don'ts

Don't Compete on Price Alone

When developing your drop-shipping business, price is not the only thing to take into account. Look for different methods to provide more value and support a higher price instead of concentrating solely on how to offer something for a lower price.

There are many strategies to demand a higher price while still making the sale, including product knowledge and experience, service, packaged deals, and free shipping.

Don't Market the Same Product that Everyone Else Is

This is crucial because price reductions happen when many companies and sellers compete to sell the same products. You also rob yourself of the opportunity to become a leader in that niche, especially if you have older competitors. You can use the Print on Demand dropshipping model to really differentiate yourself by designing your own merchandise. I will go over this in more detail later in the book.

Do Choose a Niche

Choosing a niche to sell in and honing your product knowledge and experience in that area are both significantly more sustainable business strategies. Especially considering that you can experiment with selling any type of product as a dropshipper.

Do Profit from Seasonal Goods

Since traditional stores typically don't carry enough of it out of concern for overstocking, seasonal products can be a significant source of income for you. Create a year-round merchandising schedule for when you intend to provide particular products. This way, you can guarantee what will be available well in advance of the relevant season or holiday.

Do Experiment with Product Bundling to Improve your Profit Margins

If you have several products arriving from the same warehouse, bundling can considerably lower shipping costs. So pay attention to the products your customers could want in addition to a product that is doing well but on which you don't have a large margin, and package the two together. Then, use the additional margin from the ancillary items to make up for the large product's low margin where necessary.

Some bundling Shopify apps with several great reviews are Bundle Bear by Conversion Bear and UFE Cross Sell & Upsell Bundle.

Do Market Your Knowledge

Consider the lifetime of experiences you've had thanks to your interests, passions, and hobbies. Which goods have you used the most frequently? What have you discovered utilizing these goods that most merchants are unaware of? That knowledge is to your advantage.

Do Explore Various Marketplaces

Most prosperous dropshippers today are also multichannel vendors, which means they sell their goods on various online platforms. This is important because when you limit your options to just one platform, you lose out on customers who are searching for your goods on all the other platforms. Some recommended marketplaces are Walmart Marketplace and eBay, depending on your niche.

There are other marketplaces that specialize in certain niches that you can also sell on, such as Etsy (mainly print on demand) or Newegg.com (electronics focused).

I DO NOT recommend Amazon. You compete on price mainly and Amazon does NOT protect its sellers from "competitive sabotage." I have a long bitter story regarding my experience with Amazon. Needless to say, I do not sell there currently and have not in the last 4 years.

Do Offer Top-Notch Customer Service

At every step of the process, be sure to keep the customer informed about the status of their transaction, confirming receipt and shipment dates, etc. Trust is the name of the game here, and providing excellent customer service is by far the most effective approach to get favorable comments, ratings, and reviews.

Do Test Different Shipping Rates

Why not offer a related product to your customer in a package with the original product at a somewhat higher price and then seal the deal by providing free shipping if they are already somewhat interested in it? You might be surprised at how popular this choice is since it gives the impression that customers are getting the most for their money.

In addition, you can test free shipping over a certain dollar amount. Some popular dollar thresholds are $30, $49, $59 and $99. This can sometimes increase your average order value (AOV).

Nearly 85% of all websites provide free shipping in some form. It is almost necessary to do the same to remain competitive. Another strategy is to provide free shipping above a certain dollar amount, such as "free shipping on orders over $55."

Do Improve your Product Descriptions

The fastest method to go unnoticed in a crowded market is for many shops to just duplicate the manufacturer's product descriptions and images. It could take longer to do the opposite but trust the process.

The whole idea here is to attract more views than the copied and pasted descriptions offered by the manufacturer.

If you are relaunching your dropshipping business, below are a few things to consider in addition to the foregoing.

Key Factors To Consider Before Relaunching

Is the Layout of your eCommerce Website Mobile-First?

The UX of your website should prioritize important components due to the constrained space on smaller screens. Mobile-first websites not only perform better on search engines but also take into account evolving customer preferences for designs created specifically for their preferred device.

There are several Web 2.0 (mobile first) Shopify themes available on the Shopify theme store as well as Themeforest.net. I personally have used the Ella responsive theme, but my most recent favorite is Minimoog with the Foxkit add-on and secondly the Warehouse theme.

Have you made On-Site Searches Better?

An essential aspect of the user experience is the on-site search function. Take a closer look at this functionality before launching, otherwise, your customers could abandon your site in favor of another with easier on-site searches. When deciding on a Shopify theme, find one that has a search bar that provides a great on-site search experience.

Are the Speed and Functionality of your Website up to Par?

Your web visitors could leave your page if it takes longer than 3 seconds to load. This means that there isn't much time for you to make a lasting impression before your customers make up their own minds.

In addition to pleasing users and maintaining high conversion rates, a quick-loading website also satisfies search engines, which actively place better-performing pages considerably higher in organic search results.

Have you made your Checkout Procedure more Efficient?
The majority of visitors that browse your website and add goods to their carts will not ultimately buy anything. This can be a result of unexpectedly high delivery charges, an inability to pay using their preferred method, or a lack of interest. Fortunately, there are ways to speed up the checkout procedure and make it simpler for your customers. (More to follow on this.)

Is your Website Ready to Go International?
Foreign selling has many obstacles, such as higher shipping costs, local taxes, and breaking into untapped markets, but if it allows you to establish a strong brand presence in some of the most rapidly developing countries in the world, the benefits far exceed the drawbacks.

If you prefer to sell only in your country of preference, you can still make a ton of money doing so, but it is good to consider going internationally. I have some sites that are international and some sites that are only USA based.

Are you Working with the Best Dropshipping Suppliers?
Review your suppliers' list to ensure that once you relaunch, you would only partner with the most reliable brands out there. This is very important if you are relaunching, particularly if this was an issue for your brand during your initial launch. I have a list of reliable and trustworthy dropship suppliers as well as print-on-demand suppliers that I use and swear by. I also include in that list some of the ones that have consistently proven to be unreliable and I have blacklisted them as ones NOT to use....like....ever. I will share those in a later chapter.

Are the Prices of your Products Appropriate?

This is one of the most important questions to answer when launching your dropshipping business. If you want to charge more for your products, it's best to employ the innovations and value-added services that are available to you in order to give the purchase a sense of greater value. Or, if pricing is low, consider measures to actively increase the appeal of your brand to additional customers.

As you can see there are many reasons why your shop may not be making money. You need to examine your shop with scrutiny and take all of the above factors into consideration and make the necessary updates, changes, and improvements. Only then will you be able to pinpoint the culprit and be able to fix it.

Key Takeaways

◆ A rule of thumb in the dropshipping business is to aim for your profit margin to be up to 30-40% if you get TRUE wholesale prices, which I will show you how to do.

◆ The amount of visitors to your website determines how many chances your company has to make a good first impression, provide quality sales, share your brand, and develop partnerships.

◆ A prompt and considerate answer to a customer's email or message can allay their worries and persuade them to keep doing business with you.

There is much more that you can do to increase traffic to your site is to pay attention, follow, and choose a niche for your store. These are the topics we will explore in the following chapter.

3.

Choosing A Trending Niche

We are drawn to certain crowds and interests more than others. In the business world, we often have to find the 'crowd' or industry that challenges and motivates us to grow. Put differently, we have to find and operate within our niches so that we can expand our business visions. Let's discuss this further below.

Niche Strategy

Your niche strategy is a combination of choosing your target market, identifying an unfulfilled need within that market, researching your target demographic and your existing competitors, developing a business strategy, and promoting your company to your target market. Finding your own niche matters greatly because it arms you with everything you need to serve and adjust your marketing tactics to suit the needs of your potential audience.

Business Niche: Definition.

Simply put, a business niche refers to a certain segment of interest of a larger sector that a company specializes in or focuses on. It is a gap in the market where a certain customer base or target market will value your brand's unique selling proposition (USP).

Why is it Important to Pick a Business Niche?

Figuring out your niche is a very important step in the business world because it affords you the following advantages.

You Can Build a Devoted Customer Base by Focusing on a Niche

This enables you to recognize your brand and product and to determine whether your offer meets your target audience wants. Furthermore, concentrating on a smaller demographic enables you to focus on the caliber of your service quality and build lasting relationships with your customers.

It Lessens Competition

You can set yourself apart from other existing businesses that target the larger market by entering a niche. You may concentrate on providing superior goods and services instead of having to compete with well-known brand names.

It Lowers the Price of Marketing

You can reduce your marketing and advertising costs if you know about your target market in detail. How? Well, instead of investing your resources in more general promotional activities, you'll create targeted advertisements and campaigns that are tailored to the focused interests of your audience. Additionally, niche marketing enables you to nurture more intimate connections with your customers.

It Exhibits Knowledge

Instead of offering just another generic product, you can position your brand as an authority in the sector by focusing on your chosen niche. Being recognized as an expert in this way sets you apart from other brands, draws in the right customers, and builds the credibility of your brand.

An Increase in Profit

Setting up shop in a specialist industry means that you can charge more for your goods or services. For inexperienced and older dropshippers alike, this supply and demand ratio can be exceptionally beneficial and lucrative.

Examples of Niche Markets

You can certainly designate a product as a niche business concept if you can think of one that meets one of your particular demands. There are numerous niche markets in every sector, the top of which are the following.

Weight Loss and Fitness Market

The global weight loss market makes billions of dollars in revenue yearly. What's more, fitness-related goods and services are predicted to continue to be in demand due to rising health knowledge and consciousness. Weight loss apps and social networks for daily exercises, amongst others are instances of specialty companies in the fitness and weight reduction industry.

Specialized Markets for Pet Care

The opportunity for developing niche enterprises in the ever-expanding pet market is limitless. Pet-related products, applications, training programs, grooming services, and pet insurance are examples of niche markets. Toys, snacks, and training aids are sent to pet owners as part of the PupBox subscription service, and digital pet insurance and wellness services are all lucrative examples of this niche.

Child Care Products

Many specialized enterprises that cover a previously unidentified market gap quickly become regarded as vital. Prosperous baby products today include smart baby monitors, or an AI tool that allows parents to keep an eye on their kids' internet activity.

What is a Niche Strategy?

How do you develop a business niche for your company, especially now that you can appreciate the importance of finding your own niche? Let's talk about the steps below.

Decide who your Target Customers Are

This is an important question for you to answer. Otherwise, you might find yourself grasping at straws in a matter of months. Focusing on a subject or specific interest, or solutions you are familiar with and then identifying subtopics within that subject is a solid way to figure this out.

Identify a Need that is Unfulfilled or Poorly Met

Determine market gaps by analyzing your target customers. Your products should alleviate a problem that your target market is presently facing. Be sure to pick a sector where expansion is still a possibility.

Research your Demographic

Early on in choosing your product line, it's critical to include your audience. Define your demographic by identifying your target gender, age range, and geographic location (USA, worldwide, UK), if you haven't already. You should also perform regular maintenance checks to assess your customers and competitors and allow for this to expand and evolve over time.

Update Your Business Plan

This will help you decide on a pricing strategy, explain your ideal customer, and specify exactly what you'll offer and the demand it will satisfy. Adjust your business concept to take into account what you've learned about your potential customers.

Promote your Company to your Potential Customers

Your marketing efforts should be targeted in the same way that your products fit a particular demographic. Some invaluable options for spreading your message to your potential customers include targeted advertisements using Google Shopping and Google Ads.

Identifying and Dominating a Business Niche

When attempting to locate and control your chosen niche, you need to take a few important customer factors into account. These include the following.

Easily Identifiable Customers

Customers who can be identified easily are a sign of a successful industry. As a dropshipper, your business plan is doomed if you can't group your ideal customers into a discernible division.

Customers Who are Simple to Reach

Your potential customers must be readily accessible in order for your company's specialty to be lucrative. Otherwise, your marketing efforts will be useless as the costs of locating them would overshadow all your potential gains.

A Market that is Underserved or Ignored

For a niche to truly be a thought leader in its industry, it must cater to a market that is underserved or even ignored. I advise looking at these industries' markets as prospective niches. A sizable prospective market is necessary for your business to be lucrative to be able to sell your goods and services for a profit. I recommend using google.com/trends for this research.

Is Your Niche Profitable?

There are many dropshippers today who have decided on their niches and have developed their strategies to launch, without fully understanding whether or not their chosen niche is actually profitable. For such people, success can be a laborious and time-consuming process of trial and error. Let's discuss how you can avoid a similar fate below.

How to Know if Your Niche Is Profitable

Choose Your Passion

Discovering your hobbies and interests requires time and effort. One of the most difficult activities you can take on is running a business. You will only be able to get through the difficult times if you have a true passion or interest in what you do. You would have higher chances of making a good profit as well.

Identify the Niche Market Value

The next stage is to determine the market value of the niche you have identified as potentially lucrative. You must have a clear understanding of the value of the market niche you intend to penetrate. Knowing the market value can help you estimate how much money you can expect to make from the niche. There's a good possibility you can find a profitable niche if the market value is high.

Research into Recent and Current Trends

Extensive research into trends will help you learn a lot about your future industry, particularly as each business sector's history is usually a great indicator of how successful it can get.

The good news is that it's now simpler than ever to research previous and present trends in a variety of specialty markets. All you have to do is visit Google Trends and look up your niche. Not only would you access information on as many market niches as possible, the data you get would also be free of charge.

Figure out the Problems that Must be Addressed

The people who will eventually buy your product or service must have an issue that your niche can address for them. By speaking to them through your ads, you can learn about the issues that need to be fixed.

You can also carefully browse through various discussion boards like Reddit and Quora to determine which issues are frequently brought up.

Lookup Items or Products to Sell

If you believe you can find a solution, you most likely have a niche market you can exploit. Following that, you will need to provide goods that you will sell to assist in resolving the issue. If there are numerous products available for sale, a small niche might be quite lucrative. For instance, running, swimming, yoga, and other activities are examples of sub-niches within the sports & fitness category.

Read Reviews Carefully

Reviews can help you determine whether or not your target market is willing to pay for your products. The audience's willingness to pay for the goods is the best-demonstrated by-products that have received many favorable evaluations. The amount of reviews also matters just as much as the percentage of good ones.

Assess the Competition

A critical step in figuring out whether a niche is viable or not is investigating the competitors. A sufficiently competitive niche is a sign that the subject is highly lucrative. This research would also help you determine if you can carve out any room in the niche, and how to set your company out from the competition.

Investigate Online Advertisements

Finding out whether companies are prepared to spend money on web advertising is one of the best ways to determine whether a niche market is successful. If they are, the market segment is probably quite successful.

Strong Affinities or Associations

You want a niche that has a strong connection to your target market. The likelihood of profitability in the niche increases with the strength of the association. Facebook's Audience Insights, for instance, can be used to evaluate a niche's affinity or association. It will result in improved financial outcomes for your company.

Put your Ideas to the Test

You can increase website visitors and monitor the performance of your merchandise by testing, testing, and more testing. You can determine whether your niche is indeed lucrative or whether you need to change it by testing your products. In addition, keep in mind the 80/20 rule. You will make 80% of your profits from 20% of your merchandise.

Profitable Dropshipping Niches

There are numerous profitable business opportunities in the rapidly-expanding world of dropshipping business every day. If you find your Shopify store isn't focused enough, you may consider a full revamp and focus on a new niche. Some profitable niches include the following.

Beauty

One of those markets where many customers are eager to shell out cash for items they don't always need is the beauty industry. Sales in the beauty sector are projected to reach $784.6 billion by 2027 (Common Thread Collective, 2022).

As such, if you are interested in this niche, it would be really beneficial for you to know what the most popular beauty products are right now on websites like Amazon if you want your e-commerce company to succeed.

Survival Gear

Whether the preparations are for camping, an outdoor retreat, or in anticipation of a natural disaster, I've noticed that somehow, there's always a need for survival gear. This niche is very profitable as survivalists and preppers often buy survival equipment all year round.

Pets

This niche is very profitable because people who own pets but lack the time or resources to shop around town are drawn to products like cat litter and dog food.

Additionally, people enjoy seeing their pets happy, even to the point of spoiling their pets. If this is your chosen niche, ensure that these products are always accessible so that customers can purchase from your shop.

Ladies' Clothing

Look at any department store in America today and you might understand why this niche is as profitable as it is - records billions of dollars in annual revenue. Many women enjoy shopping, especially for clothes, and so are always on the lookout for trending wear for any occasion.

Child Products

Baby items are among the top sellers, more so than any other product category (including books). There is a huge demand for distinctive baby products since parents want their kids to stand out from the crowd.

Additionally, a lot of mothers may purchase a different product if they think it will be of higher quality or safer for their kids. I have a children's baby bag store that is one of my top profit makers.

Vitamins, Herbal Remedies, and Dietary Supplements

As profitable as this niche is, you must exercise caution before getting on board. Why? Because it can be very difficult to determine a product's actual ingredients. Also, the Food and Drug Administration in the US will check out anything with a health claim (and other organizations in other countries). This means that without due diligence here, you run the risk of facing legal and other sorts of liabilities.

Gadgets

People are constantly searching for the newest gadgets and products that can simplify their life. People can find products through gadgets that they might not otherwise be able to afford. When dropshipping such devices, you should be cautious of subpar products because they often result in a higher number of returns. Naturally, this could have a negative financial impact.

Sports Products

It might be challenging to discover the ideal sports-related item without spending a lot of time reading through Amazon listings, particularly for commodities with a fierce rivalry like basketballs and soccer balls.

Here's where you enter into the picture: You can tap into a solid business concept with a high likelihood of success and ROI by opening an online store specifically targeted at this group. Golf, soccer (football), tennis, basketball, MMA, weightlifting, and fitness are common sports to consider.

Leggings and Athletic Clothing

With the popularity of athleisure, more individuals are searching for apparel that can be used for both daily activities, lounging around the house and exercises.

These days, activewear includes dresses, shorts, bra tops, and designer clothing. Keep an eye out for trends in these markets since if something sells out quickly, it often won't be available again until the next season.

Jewelry

One of those products that can leave a lasting first impression on customers is jewelry, which is also fiercely competitive. It might be difficult to tell the difference between a high-quality product and one that is subpar.

Although dropshippers have numerous options and paths to choose from, having a theme and a specific target market may make or break you. The best part is that selling dropship jewelry on social media can be simple, as long as you have good communication skills and make your customers fully aware of what they are receiving. For example, costume jewelry vs. fine jewelry.

Final Thoughts and Chapter Summary

Choosing the right niche for your shop is incredibly important as it can make or break your store. Due to its importance, let's look at some of the more important points from this chapter as a summary.

◆ A business niche is a certain segment of interest of a larger market that your company specializes in or focuses on. It is a gap in the market where a certain customer base or target market will value your brand's unique selling proposition.

◆ Your niche strategy is a combination of choosing your target market, identifying an unmet or unfulfilled need within that

market, researching your target demographic and your existing competitors, updating your business plan, and promoting
your company to your target market.

◆ Picking a business niche would boost your returns, limit your
competition, and marketing costs and help you build a loyal
customer base over time.

Choosing the right niche is a highly effective way to make your shop
even more profitable, but it is only one part of the equation. The other
is working with the right suppliers. Let's look a little deeper into this.

4.

Work With The Best Suppliers

More often than we realize, working with dishonest or disorganized suppliers ranks high on the list of reasons why our dropshipping businesses struggle to grow. This is hardly surprising, especially when you consider the impact, negative or positive, your suppliers could have on your business model in general.

Your suppliers can affect almost every component of your business, such as customer satisfaction and loyalty, the quality of your ratings, delivery schedules, quality control, and your brand's reputation as a whole.

Now I know that you can always switch bad suppliers out for more reliable ones at any point you need to but it's so much preferable to pick reliable partners upfront. But how can you do that, especially as you've probably worked with not-so-great suppliers in the past? Let's discuss this in greater detail below.

Finding Reliable Dropshipping Suppliers

It's sometimes best to use a supplier's directory if you're not sure where to start. Supplier directories are easy ways to find and/or browse a big range of suppliers in one location. Oftentimes, these directories map out all the network of suppliers you could use for your dropshipping business, grouping them by market, specialty, or the sort of products they offer.

Supplier's directories also come in handy if you are in the process of a relaunch and need fresh ideas either for new products to sell or different market niches to target.

Supplier directories might be a useful tool if you're pressed for time and prepared to spend money. You should be able to locate the main suppliers in your field easily if you already know the sector or market you want to sell in.

Before You Contact Suppliers

Now imagine that you've browsed through a supplier's directory and you've spotted some great suppliers within your chosen niche. You are all pumped up and can hardly stop yourself from reaching out to them. Still, it pays to have your business affairs as organized as possible before you dial that number or fire off those emails. Here are some things you should do before initiating contact.

You Must be Legitimate

In a bid to discourage the antics of time-wasters in the industry, most suppliers only reveal their prices to legitimate retail customers (you). As such, it pays to have your business lawfully incorporated and/or registered before contacting those great suppliers on the directory.

In addition, be sure to also get your Federal EIN (Employer Identification Number) from the IRS website. You will need your corporate papers registered with your state in order to receive your EIN. The IRS website allows you to receive your EIN online.

You generally won't need to send them your incorporation documents though, especially if all you want to do is ask a few basic inquiries, such as "Do you supply X and Y products to dropshippers?"

What they may ask you for is your reseller certificate. In the US, this is usually provided by your state. In Utah, it is my Sales Tax registration certificate. In other states, it may be called something different. What this does is allow you to charge the relevant sales tax in your state and allows you to buy from suppliers without paying sales tax yourself.

Don't count on relaunching successfully or working with the best suppliers in your niche if your business isn't recognized as a legal entity by law.

Establish your Credibility from the First Conversation you Have with Them

People with "excellent business plans" are always asking suppliers tons of questions, taking up a lot of their time, and never placing any orders. You must demonstrate how different you are from such people from the onset of your conversation with a potential supplier.

For instance, don't start off demanding discounted prices or spending hours on the phone with their sales personnel, asking complex questions. It will damage your supplier's relationship with you and quickly gain you a negative first impression.

Also, be very mindful of the way you speak. Instead of using evasive language like "I'm thinking about maybe opening a business maybe soon," be clear about your business intentions ("I am relaunching this website on February 20").

Don't be Terrified of Using your Phone

It is sometimes best to initiate contact with a potential supplier through email. Sometimes though, you'll need to pick up the phone, place a call and receive the information you need directly from your would-be supplier or a representative. Don't let this worry you.

Since suppliers frequently receive phone calls, you'd probably speak with someone who would be delighted to answer your inquiries. A good tip here is to always write out your questions in advance and consult your notes during the call. Not only would this simple trick steady your nerves, but it will also make you more confident and make the phone call much simpler for all parties concerned.

Spotting the Best Dropshipping Suppliers

If you are looking for ways to spot the best suppliers within your market or niche, you are in luck. Below are the six characteristics you should watch out for because they are all present in all the best dropshipping suppliers.

Industry Focus and Knowledgeable Employees

The best suppliers often have top-notch sales professionals who are well-informed about the company's product ranges and the industry as a whole. It's quite helpful to be able to call a person with your inquiries.

Dedicated Customer Service Personnel

Were you assigned to a specific sales representative tasked with looking after you and addressing any concerns you might have? The best suppliers tend to do this because problems can take far longer to fix if you have to speak to a different rep each time you call. It's better to have a single supplier contact that is in charge of resolving your problems.

Understands and Invests in New Technologies

While there are many reliable vendors with old websites, working with a supplier who appreciates and invests in technology will almost always turn out great for you. If your would-be supplier's website has features like real-time inventory, a thorough online catalog, customized data feeds, and online searchable purchase history, it means that they have gone the extra mile to ensure that you can optimize your business as well as your working relationship with them.

Can Process your Orders through their Wholesale Website

Although it may seem like a minor problem, processing orders takes much longer when every order must be called in or entered manually. You should be given a username and password to the suppliers website in order to access wholesale pricing.

Located Conveniently

Location is another crucial feature to examine closely before you begin your working relationship with a supplier. The reason for this is simple: your customers' orders could take a lot longer to fulfill when a supplier is situated in another country, such as AliExpress in China.

The ability to reliably guarantee quick delivery times from centrally situated suppliers, such as a supplier in your own country, can also help you maximize your profits by avoiding the delays of international shipping.

Efficient and Well-Organized

It can be challenging to determine just how capable a supplier is if you don't place any orders with them. Still, suppliers who are well-organized and efficient are also generally some of the most effective and reliable suppliers out there. I will share a list of some ot the most efficient and well organized suppliers shortly.

Finding Dropshipping Suppliers

There are several ways to identify excellent suppliers for your drop-shipping business, from directories to phone calls. Here are our top suggestions to get you going.

Talk to the Manufacturers

Pick up your phone and call up the manufacturers of the goods you want to sell. Introduce yourself, and ask them for a list of distributors they could recommend for the kinds of goods they produce. This is a great way to be sure that you're looking at reliable vendors. That is if the manufacturer does not dropship directly to your end customer.

Use Niche Scraper

A product research tool called Niche Scraper could also help you iden-tify the most popular products in your niche. Additionally, it offers dropshippers a daily selection of suppliers, products, and ad-targeting strategies that have been approved by its specialists.

Check out a Trade Show

Find out if there are any trade shows in your area. Trade exhibi-tions are a terrific way to meet your potential suppliers and see the products in person. Tickets can sometimes be expensive but you can tackle this challenge by booking ahead to buy the tickets cheaper.

Conduct Extensive Google Searches

Many wholesale dropshipping vendors still struggle with marketing. In light of this, you ought to use a variety of search keywords on Google and scroll past the first page of results. Also, don't discard a potential supplier just because their website is difficult to use. Do your best to be as open-minded as possible throughout your selection process.

Purchase from Rivals

Purchase some goods from rival dropshippers or merchants if you want to emulate them. You can discover the name of their dropshipping supplier by looking at the return address. This is a fantastic chance to research the competition and discover possible suppliers all at once.

How to Spot a Fake Dropshipping Company

Insufficient Contact Information

Most dropshipping suppliers may not have the resources or the know-how to design the best websites out there. It is, however, expected that any credible supplier website would have multiple contact information, including addresses and phone numbers. It is not advisable to trust a supplier whose website lacks all of these details.

Markets To The Public

Dropshipping suppliers set themselves apart from conventional companies by supplying the inventory to e-commerce websites that don't want to keep their inventory and handling order completion on their behalf. Any vendor that conducts their own business by marketing to the end customers directly cannot provide reasonable profit margins for you to compete directly with the supplier.

Promises to Give You High Margins

Since your supplier retains and maintains inventory on your behalf while also delivering straight to your customers, dropshipping is a very low-margin business model. As such, any supplier who promises to boost your company's earnings quickly by offering you big margins may be suspicious. These can be deceptive tactics used to lure entrepreneurs into receiving subpar goods, which will eventually result in returns from disgruntled customers. Avoid such suppliers.

Refuses To Provide You With Sample Products

It is always advisable to request samples from your future suppliers during the evaluation phase. It is advisable to set aside some of your budget to order samples. This is not only a crucial procedure to examine the product's quality, but it also serves as a check to determine the reliability of the supplier.

Samples will be reluctantly provided by fake dropshipping vendors, who may also request more time to send them (so that they have ample time to arrange for a counterfeit). These are red flags and such suppliers should be avoided at all costs.

There is something else I'd like to point out here. Since you have operated in the dropshipping business, I'd guess you've probably heard that suppliers who request monthly membership fees from dropshippers are not to be trusted. Well, I can tell you from personal experience that this isn't true, it's only an opinion.

Following such generic statements would only work to keep your business from investing in really good dropshipping wholesalers. I followed this advice myself for a while until I tested Doba, AppScenic, Syncee, and a few others.

These are some legitimate dropshipping sources that charge fees and in turn, you get true wholesale prices. For these suppliers, charging fees helps keep their platform free of fraudulent merchandise and is a barrier to those who are not serious.

Refuses To Sign Any Contracts With You
You must sign a contract with your dropshipping supplier before starting your collaboration with them. Oftentimes this is available online as you sign up. Such a contract should clearly state the terms of your working relationship with each other, as well as the procedures to follow if either party balks at their obligations at any point. If your future supplier refuses or stalls to sign the agreement, treat this as a red flag and find someone better to work with.

Middlemen Dropshippers
Sometimes, certain websites represent themselves as dropshippers when in reality, all they do is forward your order to the actual wholesalers, making them middlemen. Due to the demand of such middlemen for fees to be paid to the actual dropshipper, working with them would lower your margins. For this reason, you'd best avoid them as much as possible. Several AliExpress shops use this model.

Dropshipping calls for great prudence before relaunching. On that note, here are some of the best platforms where you can connect to the credible suppliers you need. Some are free and some are fee-based.

Best Dropshipping Vendors

Worldwide Brands

Founded in the year 1999, this platform houses some of the most established and well-known supplier directories today. Worldwide Brands guarantees genuine, high-quality suppliers as they only list suppliers who adhere to their set of rules.

The vetted suppliers ship products all across the world. There are more than 16 million approved wholesale products available in a variety of markets, including pet supplies, jewels and watches, customer electronics, home furnishings, clothing, and more.

If you want lifetime access to a reliable wholesale supplier directory and are happy to pay a fee upfront, consider using this platform.

Doba

You can use Doba's unified interface to place orders with numerous suppliers. This is not a free service, but it is worth the monthly charge. Global shipping is available; shipping costs are determined by the wholesalers you choose and the prices you specify. More than two million products on the platform have respectable profit margins. Doba has been a great option for my websites.

Wholesale2b

Wholesale2b provides real-time inventory automation and makes it very easy to import orders and track changes through your Shopify store. Products from Wholesale2b are delivered to Canada and the US. Now although product and supplier factors affect shipping timeframes, the platform offers a shipping time report that shows you the typical number of days it takes for each supplier to send products. It works best for dropshippers who want their items delivered quickly, especially within North America. However, you may not get the best wholesale prices here.

Wholesale Central

This network is ideal for dropshipping for US-based sellers because it has more than 1,400 wholesale dropshippers and more than 700,000 items. Warning: A few of the wholesalers who offer dropshipping on this platform seemed to be retailers selling to the general public at "wholesale" pricing, which is not something a dropshipping supplier would do. As a result, you might wish to exercise a little extra due diligence while using this site. In addition, you will need to contact each supplier directly from this website.

Modalyst

This is an automated vendor dropshipping site, renowned for carrying goods from well-known brands that customers adore (eg. Calvin Klein, Dolce & Gabbana). With the exemption of South American and African countries, the listed suppliers on this site can ship to over 80 nations worldwide. Product categories are broad, with an emphasis on upscale and cutting-edge labels. This platform is best suited for Shopify dropshippers who wish to add distinctive products to their stores. However, what you will find is last year's designer brands lines, not the current year. Stock can sometimes be limited as well.

AppScenic

This dropshipping platform gives users all the resources they require to increase sales anywhere and at any time. It delivers goods to Andorra, Afghanistan, Antigua & Barbuda, Antigua, Anguilla, the United Arab

Emirates, and 224 other nations. Product kinds include everything from clothing to jewelry to accessories for technology to pet items and everything in between. This is one of my favorite websites that has 3 tiers of paid access. If you go for the highest tier, you will make the most profit. When first starting with this site, I made more than $25K in the first 8 weeks. You will find true wholesale prices here.

CJDropshipping
CJDropshipping is a marketplace and directory of wholesale drop-shippers that you can use to quickly and affordably import products into your Shopify store. If you are shipping from China, CJPacket, a shipping company owned by CJDropshipping, can deliver your goods to the US in seven to twelve days if you want to pay for express ship-ping and pass that on to your customer. This is one of the exceptions I have for having local suppliers.

You may browse hundreds of millions of listings on CJDropshipping, and the products range from commonplace commodities to uncom-mon items. You can submit a request for a product that is missing from the CJDropshipping app, and the company will list it once it locates the best source. If you want a single platform to handle everything related to dropshipping, including product sourcing, order processing, order fulfillment, and a speedy shipment to the United States, you can use this platform. This is akin to getting a Chinese agent. Be aware that items run out of stock quickly, so you need to stay on top of the inventory available through CJDropshipping.

Syncee.co (not .com)
For anyone searching for a trustworthy source of pre-screened drop-shipping vendors based in the US, Canada, Europe, UK, Australia, Asia,

and several other places, Syncee.co is a terrific choice. It provides a completely automated shipping method for managing products in an easy way for ecommerce websites. It's key benefits include:

◆ Availability of millions of profitable products in 400 different categories.

◆ reliable, well screened providers with quick shipping from around the globe.

◆ Ease of bulk expansion of your product lines.

◆ Access to bulk-customizable price settings, including rounding rules and price margin.

◆ You can set filters for what gets uploaded because the platform has flexible settings for products and catalogs.

◆ Ease of communication with your supplier within the app, and so on.

Final Thoughts and Chapter Summary

Working with the best suppliers is a careful balance of finding what you need for the right price and from the right people. Let's review some of the important points.

◆ Your suppliers can affect almost every component of your business, such as customer satisfaction and loyalty, the quality of your ratings, delivery schedules, quality control, and your brand's reputation as a whole.

◆ Supplier directories are easy ways to find and/or browse a big range of suppliers in one location. It's always best to use a supplier's directory if you're not sure where to start.

◆ Ensure that your business is registered and affairs are as orga-nized as possible before you start reaching out to potential suppliers.

◆ Any vendor that conducts their own business by marketing to the customers directly should be investigated thoroughly to determine legitimacy.

Although you can have the right niche and be working with the best suppliers, your store may be suffering if you don't have the right look. A professional-looking design for your website is key. In the following chapter, we will go over how you can create a professional website interface.

5.

Creating a Professional Store and Redesigning Your Website

Did you know that about 50% of potential business transactions are lost because customers on eCommerce sites have a hard time finding what they are looking for? (Forrester, 2012). In fact, this research also found that if customers in the US have questions regarding a product and can't access an answer quickly, a minimum of 45% of them will give up on the purchase. Conversely, about 49% of online buyers are most likely to buy even more products, and 86% of them are willing to pay extra when they have simpler and better buying experiences on websites (Draper, 2022).

Common Problems

The above figures show that if you want to generate more sales or grow your earnings, you must make your web design simple enough for your customers to navigate through and find the products they

want easily. Below are some common problems associated with drop-shipping websites that could result in little web traffic.

Lack of SEO Optimization

Your page will have a greater likelihood of being discovered whenever a potential customer searches for the services you provide if it has strong SEO on each product page. Search engine optimization calls for keyword research, skillful writing, creative design, as well as technical expertise. It also requires thorough knowledge of your target customer. You can have the most beautiful website in your chosen niche but without SEO optimization, your customers wouldn't know it exists.

It is Not Compatible with Mobile Devices

Cell phones account for a sizable portion of all global internet traffic, as more customers choose their mobile for greater convenience when purchasing. Your website must therefore work just as well on mobile devices as it does on desktops. Choosing a mobile responsive Shopify theme is key to this.

You have Poor-Quality Images or Information on your Site

With low-quality content or images, customers won't be eager to interact with your website. This is because the message conveyed is that you are not a professional company therefore, are not trustworthy. Analyze your images and text copy on each of your product listings to determine if your images and text convey enough information to answer the questions your potential customers may have.

Technical Difficulties (such as delayed page load time)

These days, with the press of a button, a customer can quickly order items from anywhere in the world and have them delivered the following day. If it takes a long time for your site to load, usually longer than three seconds, it's likely that your customers won't come back. Use page speed insights found at https://developers.google.com/speed.

No Obvious Call to Action

You must direct site visitors to a specific course of action to retain their attention and assist them to explore your site. This could be as simple as adding "Buy Now" to your product listing.

Incomplete or Inadequate Product Descriptions

The best product information or descriptions include as many details as possible on the item's functionality, appearance, size, speed, warranty, and other factors. When such information is missing or unclear, the features of your product become difficult to understand.

Lack of a Strong Sales Pitch

Customers are interested in learning more about the characteristics of the goods they're thinking about buying than just the numbers and qualities. How will the item be useful to them? How is it superior to what they could buy from another website? Without providing clear answers to these questions, you may not attract enough sales.

False or Absent Customer Reviews

Faking product reviews on your site is a guaranteed way to chase off your customers. Always be transparent. Allow customers to evaluate and critique your products. If there are negative reviews, look into the issue rather than trying to hide it. Always respond to negative reviews, publicly if possible. A great review app for Shopify is Judge.me. There is a free version and a paid version. Once you start getting reviews, you can upgrade to the paid version, which is highly recommended.

Additional Charges

A common cause of cart abandonment is unexpectedly large additional fees, such as hidden shipping charges. Don't only mention the shipping costs at the end of the transaction. And whatever you do, don't tack on any extra fees.

Inadequate Tracking or Logistical Problems

When order monitoring systems are reliable, they can usually resolve problems with uncertainties. customers would be disappointed with the whole service on your site and evaluate you negatively if they didn't know the precise wait time for their orders, the delivery schedules, and where their goods are at all times. There are Shopify apps that provide this and more.

Having a Rigid Policy about Returns

Unless you don't believe in the quality of your goods, there is no reason to not make your return policy as lenient as possible. Flexible return policies on your products foster trust and make life considerably simpler for those few shoppers who might return an item, increasing your chances of keeping them as customers.

Insufficient Assistance and No Real-Time Chat Option

Would-be buyers have a bunch of inquiries, particularly if the characteristics and descriptions of your products are not adequately presented. The more your customers feel unaided in this, the greater the chances of them leaving your site and never returning.

What Customers Want

Your customers want you to provide them with a better user, and customer, experience. This is the key to increasing your business sales and volume. You just have to look at the statistics of your site, and the questions you directly receive from customers as often as possible. This will paint you a complete picture of their needs, and expectations, some of which include:

Features That Work on Mobile

This is essential when designing any online store today because the majority of buyers prefer to shop on their mobile devices. To improve your engagement rate while also maintaining customer satisfaction, make sure your website design is seamlessly adjusted for the size and form of phones.

Various Methods of Payment

Add alternatives for payment processors like PayPal, or Shopify Pay in addition to providing credit and debit card choices. Customers find the provision of more payment options incredibly convenient. To entice customers to buy, you may also provide apps that allow for "buy now, pay later" features such as Klarna.

Continuous Customer Service

One of the features on your eCommerce website should be a chatbot that is available every hour of the day, every day, to assist customers. Some great free or low-cost options here are: Shopify Inbox, Facebook Messenger, or Tidio.

Make Use of Customer Testimonials and Reviews

With thousands of customers trusting other customers' testimonials as much as they would trust recommendations from their friends, reviews are essential for any successful online business today. They are especially important when you consider that your customers won't have the chance to see a product in person, and so can only rely on what previous buyers have shared about their experience with your company.

User Features and Discounts

Customers prefer to believe they are receiving an excellent deal and are being held to a different standard from other customers. Sending customized special offers to your devoted customers is a way to make them feel appreciated and special.

Detailed Product Descriptions

Offer thorough product descriptions with details on the size, texture, color, components, and country of origin. Offer top-notch product photography that displays the item from all angles, including, when applicable, pictures of models wearing the products.

Relaunching Checklist

Relaunching your online store can feel overwhelming, particularly when you are rebranding your company. Below is a simple guide to point you in the right direction as you go.

Specify the Main Goal for the Redesign of your Website

A goal provides a benchmark by which you may assess the necessity of each feature. Smart and realistic goals (for instance: increasing your site loading speed by 50 percent) will help you better coordinate your relaunching efforts. Here's how to choose the right goals for your site.

Make a List of the Issues with your Current Website

This is an important step because you must first be aware of the most urgent problems with your current website. To recognize the current issues your site grapples with, you should follow the next steps.

Get a Heatmap App such as Lucky Orange or Hotjar

These paid apps will help you understand how and why your customers interact with your website the way they do. With access to such information, you would be able to influence and enhance the user experience for your customers, as well as your site's overall functionality.

Perform a Technical Audit

You can identify the weak links in your site's general structure, accessibility concerns, and subpar site performance, by doing technical audits using tools like Google Lighthouse or a journey-mapping tool like Hotjar. Assemble the issues to determine which ones will have the biggest effects on your website when fixed.

Analyze Rival Businesses or Aspiring Shopify Dropshipping Online Stores.

Assessing the experience of your target customers on your competitors' sites might help you decide what to emphasize for your web relaunch. There are various approaches to this analysis but you can run site audits and study customer feedback as a starting point.

Come up with a Practical Budget

To understand what you can achieve with your resources, you need to have a realistic budget. This would keep you from overspending or making impromptu cuts to the essential functionality and integrations of your website.

Listing the Features and Integrations you Must Have in your New Site

As you list out the features your new site cannot do without, don't forget to include the cost of those elements in your budget. Depending on the type of service you would like to give your customers, the features on this list could evolve. And that's okay, let them.

Research Shopify Themes in the Shopify Theme Store or Themeforest.net

If you're planning to build the framework for your new website on Shopify, you don't need to consult a web design company to learn more about the process. In fact, I don't recommend Shopify owners to get a design company or outsource this. The Shopify themes are really easy to use.

My favorite themes are on themeforest.net. I love the Warehouse theme, the Minimog theme and the Ella theme, but not as much lately for the Ella theme. I have switched to the Warehouse theme because it mimics the Amazon layout.

Compare Your Existing Budget With Your Projected Spending

It is not unusual for dropshippers looking to relaunch their sites to end up investing more resources in the project than they had originally anticipated. Having an actual money management technique that works alongside your psychology instead of against it would be highly effective in this process.

It is more productive to develop spending guidelines for yourself than to create a budgeting plan which only limits your spending. Since there are so many various expenses to take into consideration (for your brand as well as your personal life), your budget might at times seem like some mathematical rule and prove increasingly tasking to stick to.

As such, the smart play is to realign your budget with practical strategies of achieving your goals upfront. Set out the practical changes you would make to your personal life to accommodate any unforeseen expenses along the way. For instance, if you order take-out daily, you could start cooking your own meals a few days a week to cut down on that cost and shift your savings to your business budget.

Begin the Site Redesigning

There are three major steps that make up the actual site redesign process.

The Content Phase

This is where you assemble all your website's necessary content assets, such as product photographs, homepage copy, logos, and brand images, and a branding style. Since you currently have a site, assess your current site features to figure out which could be reused and which needs to be replaced for your redesign. For instance, you could update your brand's colors or compile better or newer photographs of your products as needed.

The Design Phase

During this phase, you would need to decide on your new Shopify theme. My favorite themes from Themeforest.net are Warehouse and Minimog (with Foxkit). Be sure to purchase the additional time for support. I have researched site layouts and the bigger sites like department stores, Amazon, Wayfair...they all have a large search bar across the top and a very small menu bar. If you do not like Warehouse or Minimog, be sure to get a theme that has a good search bar.

The Development Phase

During this stage, you are adding in your brand colors, deciding on your Shopify widgets and how your homepage will look with your theme. You will most likely need to go through the tutorial videos of your Shopify theme to learn how it interacts with Shopify and how to use the themes widgets to your advantage.

Relaunch and Evaluation

Once the redesigning is complete, you must verify that your website functions as it should. As you can imagine, there is absolutely nothing to be gained from having the most beautifully designed website in the world if its features don't perform as planned. Fortunately, there are a few things to keep in mind to make sure your website relaunch goes smoothly.

Check for functionality

Confirm that the features of the website function as you intended by checking and using them yourself. Run through each form, whether it's for a purchase or a contact, using data unrelated to your company (such as a backup email address) to make sure it functions as intended. Verify that all links lead to the appropriate information and pages and that no links are damaged. Check that checkboxes, buttons, and dropdown menus work as intended by testing them.

Test Performance

Verify that your site is operating at its best performance level by looking at how it functions overall. Check the speed of the page load, your website's performance, and how your website handles massive amounts of data. The data you collect from all these would show you how your website would perform over an extended period.

Compatibility Testing

Test your website's compatibility with various hardware, browsers, and operating systems. Examine how the website's graphics look on various devices. Fortunately, this can be done right within the Shopify theme dashboard.

Review Content

Eliminate any dummy text, verify picture locations and sizes, verify the brand's colors and letter sizes, and make sure you use alt tags to optimize photos. In addition, you will need to compress your images to improve site load speed. I use the Shopify app called Crush.pics by Space Squirrel Ltd. You can access it through the Shopify app store.

Review your Heat Maps

When standard analytics aren't exact enough about what you should do, your heat maps will help you focus on specific user issues and in making the necessary adjustments to your website. If everything checks out well, you can begin making preparations for your relaunch.

Final Thoughts and Chapter Summary

Your website is the first impression you give to your prospective customers. But remember that even though you have to keep it professional looking you also need your store to represent you and the essence of your brand.

◆ About 49% of online buyers are most likely to buy even more products (Forrester, 2012), and 86% of them are willing to pay extra when they have simpler and better buying experiences on websites (Draper, 2022)

◆ A good website must perform properly to generate sales, as well as be aesthetically attractive and informative.

◆ Your customers want you to provide them with a better user, and customer, experience. This is the key to increasing your business sales and volume.

◆ Having smart and realistic goals are important when redesigning your website for a relaunch not only because they are attainable, but also because they would coordinate your team efforts in a more holistic way.

Once you've nailed down the image and look of your store, it is time to focus on how your customers will interact with the website and your products. We'll discuss this in the next chapter of this book so stick with me.

6.

Features and Integrations

Since you've dropshipped products before, I'm sure you can attest to the fact that advertising is essential in getting customers to visit your website in the first place. But what happens when a potential customer visits your page and isn't impressed with your products? Is there a way to improve that? Let's discuss this and other integrated topics below.

Reviews and Ratings

Online reviews are crucial for every business that operates in the digital sphere when it comes to attracting customers and upholding a good reputation. Let's talk about this in greater detail.

Who reads reviews posted online?

Short answer: practically everyone. In fact, 84% of prospective customers regard these reviews as highly as they would a personal suggestion (Bloem, nd). As you can expect, this means that online reviews have immense value. For context, the average customer is willing to pay 31% extra at a store with stellar reviews (Saleh, 2022).

Online reviews are crucial for your dropshipping business because they:

1. Increase sales: This is because they are believed to be accurate 12 times more often than other forms of marketing. (Charlton, 2012).

2. Establish trust: Reading several positive reviews on your site would make your customers believe and trust your brand. More customers are 63% more likely to purchase from your business as a result. (Malamut, 2016).

3. Assist SEO efforts: When customers search for terms connected to your store online, your brand name will show up fast and they are more likely to notice your favorable reviews.

4. Assist customers in making decisions. For instance, a product may appear in an image to be too small to fulfill customer needs, but customer reviews that precisely describe the size of such an item can reassure a hesitant buyer.

5. Facilitate problem-solving: For instance, if a dozen reviews on your site appreciate your products but criticize your delivery process, it may be time to sit up and pay attention to that area of your business.

Maximizing the Advantages of Internet Reviews

Knowing why reviews are advantageous and knowing how to take advantage of them are two different things. Let us discuss how you can maximize your reviews further.

Raise Brand Recognition

Strong reviews from Google and other review sites, for instance, can guarantee that customers will find your brand at the top of the list when they search for businesses in your sector.

Choose Keywords that Best Describe your Goods and Services

By reading reviews, you can gain insight into the terms and expressions that your customers use most frequently and fine-tune them into your brand's keywords to further improve your SEO results.

Techniques for Obtaining Reviews Online

Request Reviews

Sometimes all it takes is a simple request to convince a customer to post a review. Simply asking for feedback—whether on your payment page, as a pop-up after purchase, or as an email request after an item delivery has been confirmed—can make a significant difference. You can automate this process within the paid version of Judge.me.

Make it Simple for customers to Submit Reviews

To facilitate customer reviews, provide links to your Facebook, Google My Business, and any other relevant review sites in promotional emails and on your website.

Offer Incentives to your customers

Offering discounted prices and free shipping in return for reviews can be a successful strategy because customers adore these benefits. The advantages of having a strong base of reviews would much outweigh the expense to you. Again, this can be automated through the paid version of Judge.me.

Distribute Customer Questionnaires

Sending a follow-up email after a sale can provide you with useful feedback you can use to improve your website by asking customers to score aspects such as site navigation, the checkout process, shipment time, and product quality.

Respond to Feedback from Customers

Responses to reviews are one way that customers can feel heard. A simple "Thank you!" can make a customer feel valued and cared for. It might even prompt them to change their negative reviews to positive ones.

Automate your Request for Reviews

Using the paid version of Judge.me or similar Shopify app allows messages to be tracked to site visitors, and you can program an automated message to be sent out within a few days after the estimated delivery of their order. Be sure that the review does not get sent before they receive their order. If that happens, your customer may give an angry bad review. These strategies demand little effort from you but can yield significant profits.

Earn Online Testimonials on the Most Reliable Review Websites

Positive reviews are always welcome, some of them are more useful than others. The best sources for gathering online reviews are those mentioned below.

Google Reviews

Google reviews are perhaps one of the most important channels because of the part they play in Google's algorithms. Google considers user ratings for establishing search engine rankings; reviews make up about 9% of the overall algorithm (Podium, 2022).

Yelp! User Reviews

Yelp! employs a secret algorithm to prefer some ratings over others, in contrast to Google and Facebook, which display all reviews. This in itself provides more weight to reviews posted by users who have a significant online presence or useful information to contribute than to new accounts with brief comments. This is more often used for brick and mortar businesses that are also online.

Reviews on Facebook
Facebook has had a review program for a while. Not only can customers share their reviews, but they can also offer suggestions and highlight the stronger points of the company.

Online Reviews for Specialized Products.
For those in smaller areas, reviews may be found anywhere from communities like Reddit to personal blogs, and in many situations, these posts are really helpful.

Upselling

This is a sales tactic used to convince customers to buy costlier, or premium versions of the items they initially set out to buy for several additional benefits. Aside from generating more revenue for you, upselling also comes in handy in situations when the you merely wishes to expose the customer to other goods they may not have ordinarily considered.

Why is Upselling Important?
Upselling helps retailers build stronger relationships with their customers. If the goal is to make your customers feel like they've gotten the best deal possible while at the same time improving your Average Order Value (AOV). You can accomplish this by recommending premiums, updates, or add-ons that will ultimately add more value to their purchase. Upselling will prove to be a customer satisfaction strategy that also brings in more revenue.

It's simpler to upsell to current customers than to get new ones. This is a simple gain for many eCommerce companies looking to quicken their growth and boost their bottom line.

Overall, by making it simple for customers to do business with you, you can be sure that they will keep coming back for me.

Best Upselling Techniques
Three easy upselling tactics you can incorporate in your dropshipping business to make more profit are:

1. Displaying premium suggestions in the sidebar or at the bottom of the item or subcategory page (sometimes both) so that customers consider those before placing their orders.

2. While your customers are making their purchases, use pop-up notifications to advertise your premium recommendations on the shopping page, during the checkout process, or embedded in the abandoned cart reminder emails you send them afterward.

3. Make full use of customized follow-up emails after a sale to persuade customers to upgrade their products with the appropriate add-ons.

Other Best Upselling Practices to Try Are:

1. Encouraging upsells by offering discounts to visitors who spend more money on your website (e.g., offer free shipping or a discount on future purchases).

2. Using side-by-side comparisons to prove the superiority of the premium product.

3. Pricing the premium product reasonably, customers rarely pay more than 25% of what they had originally intended for an upgrade.

4. Recommending available alternatives without being forceful. Your customers should still have ample leeway to make their own decisions.

5. Encouraging customers to buy quickly by providing them with real-time stock updates ("just 7 products left") or a reminder that the offer is only valid for a short period.

Upselling Examples Include the Following:

1. An airline suggesting that an economy passenger upgrades to business class for some added perks.

2. A chef recommended that a diner pay an extra sum for the improved experience of having more chicken or seafood in their salad.

3. When the most basic version of a smartphone app is offered for free, but access to its premium would require paying a fee, and so on.

Steps Involved in Upselling

Increase Customer Loyalty and Trust

To begin with, you can do this by acting as a consultant rather than a salesperson. You must:

1. Completely understand your products. A customer can lose faith in your brand if you aren't able to respond to their questions satisfactorily or resolve specific problems.

2. Provide advice based on customers' preferences. If a customer feels pressured into purchasing something they don't need, they may become hostile. Show them how completing the purchase would benefit them but let them make the final decision.

3. Prioritize customer service. Remember that a good customer experience can make the difference between whether your offer for them to go premium is accepted or rejected.

Learn Your Customers' Needs and Expectations

This will boost their confidence in your company, as well as enable you to put yourself in their position and better foresee their demands. This knowledge comes from the research I mentioned earlier.

Make Personalized Suggestions for your Customers

Making the proper recommendations is essential to upselling effectively, and you should use the information you've learned about your customer to do so. To do this successfully, it's best to:

1. Recognize the needs and wants of the customer. Even though it can seem to be to your brand's advantage to provide as many offers as possible, keep your premium recommendations to a minimum so as not to overwhelm or confuse your customers.

2. Upsell but don't oversell. Suggesting upgrades that are excessively pricey compared to the base purchase could turn off the buyer. A rule of thumb here is that an upsell shouldn't raise the whole price by more than 25%.

The Best Way to Spot Upselling Opportunities

Engage with Customers by Posing Open-Ended Questions

When they discuss their demands, think about if a product or service is already available on the market to cater to those needs. If yes, how can you improve it? If not, how can you create one?

Look into Potential Methods to Enhance your Current Offering

What current products do your customers buy the most from you? Can you upgrade the product in any unique way? Can you improve shipping times?

Assess the Major Sources of your Income

Knowing the products that make your business the most money can help you determine your customer's demands and the most effective way to strategically upsell such items to them.

Ascertain the Uses and Prices of the Products in your Market Sector

For instance, you might not see many possibilities to upsell college students on the business suite if you are marketing a software tool to them. On the other hand, if you were to offer a more comprehensive package, you could be able to give students a discount.

Use Online Resources at your Disposal to Learn More about your customers

Since it's primarily a way to assuage demand, upselling should occur almost naturally. The best method to spot upselling chances is to stay knowledgeable about customers' needs from a range of perspectives.

Upselling Strategies

Techniques that Could be Used to Improve your Upselling Chances Are:

1. Delivering on your promises to keep your customers happy. Upselling depends on maintaining customers' contentment, and keeping your promises is a big part of that.

2. Ensuring that your customers understand the value and the added benefits of your premium recommendations.

3. Using upselling to help with customer care problems. Once a problem has been identified, upselling can be used to make things even better.

4. Removing as many risks as possible for your customers. Customers are more inclined to buy and have faith in your product or service when a free trial or money-back guarantee is offered.

5. Maintaining good relationships with your customers to foster trust and loyalty. The more faith your customers have in you, the more likely they are to buy the products you recommend.

Cross-Marketing

Cross-marketing is a form of advertising in which two or more companies work together to market their goods or services. It works by uniting firms to aid in their expansion into wider markets.

How does it work?

Through cross-marketing, businesses can work together to develop marketing strategies that will support each other in achieving their objectives. For instance, BMW and Louis Vuitton worked together to introduce the BMW i8. For the new automobile, Louis Vuitton created a four-piece collection of bags and suitcases. Since both businesses have customers with comparable demographics and socioeconomic statuses, the cross-sell was successful. Both businesses were able to expand their reach and notoriety as a result of the partnership. Other cross-marketing collaboration examples are discussed below.

iStock with Adobe and Invision

The stock photo website iStock teamed with Adobe and Invision. The collaboration made iStocks images easily accessible for purchase in Invision and Adobe's app. Users of Invision and Adobe were thus able to access high-quality stock pictures and increase the revenue of all parties to the collaboration.

Spotify and Uber
Spotify and Uber worked together to make Spotify music accessible in Uber journeys. The collaboration improved the waiting experience for Uber's customers while giving Spotify access to its audience.

Starbucks and Niantic
Starbucks partnered with Niantic after their augmented reality game Pokémon Go became a huge success. Starbucks made a drink with a Pokémon motif, and every Starbucks shop appeared in the game. Through the partnership, Starbucks was able to increase sales by capitalizing on the game's popularity. Niantic was also able to provide users of the Pokémon video game with a better overall experience.

Cobbler's Choice and Thursday Boot Company
The Thursday Boot Company offers fashionable boots and footwear. They collaborated with Cobbler's Choice, a company that offers high-end leather cleansers and brushes for caring for shoes. Each brand complemented the other and catered to the target market of the other.

Benefits of Cross-marketing

1. Improved brand recognition and awareness. This can be a goal for businesses that are searching for fresh ideas.

2. Sales expansion. The more you understand the needs of your customers and cross-sell to fulfill them, the more you can expand your sales.

3. Increased loyalty and trustworthiness. customers will trust your advice the more your brand is recognized within your niche.

4. Saves costs for advertising. When brands work together toward a common goal, their responsibilities, and advertising expenses are often split equally. This means that you can experiment with some sophisticated promoting strategies to attract more customers to your business.

5. Increasing the variety of products. This is typical of sportswear and athleisure businesses. This in turn would generate more awareness about the businesses and boost their sales.

6. Creating lasting partnerships. The collaborating brands in a cross-selling arrangement often end up with stronger bonds not just to each other, but to their customers as well.

How to Find The Best Cross-Marketing Partners

1. Decide on a goal. Be specific, and clear about your main goal. For instance, would you need your would-be partner to promote your business through their email campaigns or social media posts? Is the goal to release a specific premium product to grow your target demographic?

2. Assess your target audience carefully. Your chances of understanding the true worth of your product would increase with the level of information you have. This in turn would help you know the kind of partners you need to improve your brand.

3. Begin to research extensively about possible partners. Keep in mind that the goal of cross-marketing is collaboration, not competition. Make sure you have a compelling offer before approaching these businesses.

4. Sign a contract to ensure that all terms are met and to safeguard both parties. It ought to outline all of the responsibilities of both businesses as well as your expectations and financial constraints.

Now that you know all about cross-selling, here are the must-haves for your website:

1. Product filtering and sorting. This function would help you find products more easily, which is essential for the success of your business.

2. Wishlist. This would increase traffic to your website, and help you to understand your customers' preferences better. This is available in the themes I mentioned earlier.

3. Related items. With this, if a customer can't locate the item they're looking for, they might discover related items which will prompt them to place an order.

4. Shopify payments. Help your customers feel as secure as possible during the checkout process by providing for the use of credit cards, PayPal, Amazon Pay, Apple, Google Pay, Klarna (pay in 4 installments) and other payment methods.

5. Integration of fraud detection technologies. In light of the high rate of eCommerce fraud today, you can make your customers feel safe by incorporating tools like multi-step identity verification, and a real-time insights interface to protect their information. If you are selling products above $500, I recommend the app Clearsale.

6. Setting up shipping information comprises picking the best shipping options, which you may not have alot of choice in for dropshipping, offering insurance, and tracking shipments. Take this seriously.

7. Online chat. By relieving the stress of waiting on hold or for an email response, live chats demonstrate to your current and potential customers that you value their time.

8. Integration of marketing tools. Marketing automation streamlines numerous tasks that were previously handled by marketers. This would make it much easier for you to offer top-notch customer service.

9. SMS and email integration would make it simpler to keep your customers informed about your products and send them promotions. I have used the Shopify Omnisend app.

10. Google Analytics connection will make it easier for you to swiftly gather the necessary data on customer behavior and habits.

11. FAQ page. The presence of an FAQ page on your eCommerce website is yet another crucial element to consider. For

instance, your FAQs area will not only give your customers the most recent information, but also a ton of solutions to any questions they could have.

Final Thoughts and Chapter Summary

Making your website one that your customers will want to interact with is imperative if you want a successful store. After all, without customer interaction, how will you increase sales? As we have explored, there are several ways you can invite your customers to do this.

◆ Your online reviews would help you attract more customers and enforce a good reputation.

◆ If your goal is to make your customers feel like they've gotten the best deal possible by recommending premiums, updates, or add-ons that will ultimately add more value to their purchase, upselling will prove to be a customer satisfaction strategy that also brings in more revenue.

◆ Cross-marketing is a form of advertising in which two or more companies work together to market their goods or services. It works by uniting firms to aid in their expansion into wider markets.

These are some general interactions that customers can have through your site. But there are some specific interactions that you need to try to incorporate into your store site. We will examine some of these more specific interactions in the following chapter.

7.

High Ticket Dropshipping and Print On Demand

The conventional dropshipping business model focuses on selling inexpensive, high-volume goods to move many of them. A major drawback of this though is having low-profit margins, which could make any gains take longer to materialize. A possible solution to this is high-ticket dropshipping. Let's discuss this in more detail below.

What Is High Ticket Dropshipping, and How Does It Work?

Selling high value products is the main focus of high-ticket dropshipping. These are typically products ranging from $200 and above. High-ticket items give you more substantial profit margins and broader pricing options.

Low vs. High Ticket Dropshipping

Dropshipping low-ticket products work because of its high turn-over and more affordable products. Dropshipping high-ticket goods, however, you'd experience a constant stream of sales if you sell in a profitable niche backed up with an efficient marketing approach. Here, your target market is much smaller and after considering the entire value of the item, have no qualms about paying the higher prices. There is also far less rivalry in this dropshipping model than in the more conventional one because most dropshippers shy away from it.

Benefits of Dropshipping High-End Products

Maximum adaptability

You probably know from experience that being an entrepreneur gives you some freedom to manage your day better. Dropshipping high value items allows you to make fewer sales with higher profits.

Reduced Customer Support Volume

You only attend to a manageable number of customers when you sell high-value goods. This means that you would respond to complaints better, as opposed to low-ticket dropshipping businesses where customers are so many that it is much more difficult to manage and takes up much more of your time.

How It All Works

This dropshipping model is similar to the traditional dropshipping business model. The biggest distinction is in the types of goods you'll be selling. Finding the ideal niche, and a dependable supplier is essential since it will have a big impact on how successful your business is.

Mistakes To Avoid:

1. Attempting to sell distributors' low-margin goods. You should make a significant profit when dropshipping high-ticket items. Selling products from suppliers who offer poor margins will, therefore, defeat the point of operating this business model.

2. Googling "[niche] dropshippers". As popular as this is, this type of research frequently lacks depth. Let's go over how to use Google to identify vendors below.

How to Locate High-Margin Vendors

There are several sources I have discovered through my own trial and error process over the last few years. In the beginning, I avoided the paid access to dropship suppliers, however I tried one and I made over $30,000 in 8 weeks because they offered true wholesale prices. Yep, even competitive against Walmart and Amazon. Some of the main ones I have tried and have proven to really work for me are:

◆ AppScenic
◆ Syncee
◆ Doba (be careful - some of the products here have higher prices)
◆ Worldwide Brands (does not offer products, but a directory of contacts to dropship suppliers)

How to Choose High-Ticket Items

Be particular by choosing products with high-profit margins. It's best to choose a product with a large margin so that your business would

remain profitable over the long term. The higher your margins, the greater your gains will be.

Avoid markets with lots of competition. Since there often isn't a lot of competition with the higher ticket products, this approach will help you attract potential customers attention to your brand more selectively.

Best Niche Markets For Dropshipping High-End Items

Tech Gadgets

This is a smart choice if you're searching because technology isn't going anywhere for years to come. If anything, it may grow even bigger than it currently is. For instance, there is a sizable market for drones, and many people are interested in them.

Garden, Home, and Pets

The COVID-19 pandemic made many people value their homes more. Selling household necessities like furniture and certain electrical appliances can be a great opportunity to add to your business. Here you can choose expensive items like steam showers, kitchen islands, greenhouses, massage chairs and more.

Hobbies, Games, and Sports

This field has a ton of lucrative subcategories. A wine cooler, humidors, football tables, kegerators, and other high ticket equipment are some examples.

Office, Business, and Industrial

This niche is constantly expanding, so there will always be room for you to offer your goods. This group of products includes standing desks, pressure sealers, card cutters, and whiteboards, to mention but a few.

Lifestyle Niche

Countless products fall under this category; some instances are jewels, expensive bikes, and more.

Top Niches For High-End Products

Home Improvement

The COVID-19 pandemic forced most people across the globe to remain at home for months at a stretch, and more customers today want home furnishings that could provide extreme comfort. Such products include thermal showers, lighted mirrors, electrified fireplaces, massage chairs, etc.

Expensive Hobby Items

Opening a hobbyist shop is a smart move since it's easy to capitalize on high-demand periods, particularly in the summer for items like paddle boards and surfboards. Some items within this niche even sell throughout the year, eg., electric skateboards.

Kitchen Equipment and Fixtures

Items like espresso machines and kitchen islands fall under this category. Espresso machines in particular are fantastic products since you can market them to companies as well as to other spaces.

Electrical Devices such as Cameras

Camera sales have been brisk as a result of rising public interest in photography, cinematography, and editing videos. The products in this category range from drones to polaroid cameras, DSLRs, adventure cameras, and more.

Other great high-ticket dropshipping items are Garden Hammock, Remote-Control Hamster Truck, Ultralight Camping Tent, Pool Cover, Prestige Floor Fan, Pedal Go-Kart, Aluminum Solar Umbrella, Cat Tower Condo, Queen-Sized Bed, Stand-Up Paddle Board, Solar LED Garden Lamp, Assemble-At-Home Garden Shed, 3D Printer, Safe, and Car Roof Rack.

Print on Demand: A Low-Risk Way To Sell Products

Print-on-demand services enable you to produce customized goods at a portion of the cost of doing it yourself. Let's discuss this further below.

What is Print-on-Demand and How Does it Work?
When you engage with a supplier of certain products to personalize those items and sell them on an on-demand basis using your brand and your designs, you are operating a print-on-demand business. Here, your supplier takes care of every aspect of the sale, including digital printing, order fulfillment, and shipment.

You can use the print-on-demand business model to:

1. Test a new line of products or company ideas without taking the risks associated with purchasing inventory by using print-on-demand services. It also works well as a side business.

2. Earn money from an established customer base. (eg. doing POD as a YouTuber).

3. Print one-off or small batches of print-on-demand products for a specific market (for example, t-shirts for persons who are extremely passionate about long-distance running).

Is Print on Demand Still Profitable in 2022?
Absolutely! A 2018 survey from IBM and the National Retail Federation found that over half of Gen Z customers want products that are specifically curated to their preferences. The US alone has about 70 million Gen Zs. The situation is such that by 2025, the market for personalized T-shirts alone is anticipated to reach $10 billion. Also, the estimated size of the global POD market in 2021 was $4.91 billion, and it is anticipated to grow to $6.17 billion in 2022. (GrandView, 2022). This means that you have a ton of options to make your designs into actual financial gains. After all, supply always follows demand, right?

High Ticket Print on Demand

These are POD products that can give you much higher profit margins than your traditional POD products, such as mugs and t-shirts. This also means that you can spend more on ads to make more sales and still be profitable especially as there is less competition. Here are examples of high-ticket POD products: Print on Demand Wireless Bluetooth headphones, wireless charging stands, custom fleece throws, wireless Bluetooth speakers, combat boots, sneakers, leather handbags, and more.

The bottom line here is that these products cost more, there is an even higher profit margin for you, and there's far less competition than mugs and t-shirts. You don't have to ignore other staple POD products (T-shirts, hoodies, mugs, cell phone cases, etc) to sell these high-ticket products exclusively from your store. A better idea is to slowly introduce them not just to make more money, but also to show your customers products that are new and unique.

Steps to Add POD to Your Business

Come up with Ideas and Designs for Your POD Business

This would help you define your style and learn what and how you enjoy creating. For instance, if you're motivated to develop a collection of colorful leaf patterns, you might experiment with florals in a way that will make your products visually appealing. To get started, you can buy patterns and images from my favorite source creativefabrica.com.

Once you have some patterns or designs, you can use canva.com to change them around a bit, or change the colors to make the designs your own.

If you find you are not a designer, you can hire a designer on fiverr. com to create designs for you.

Post Your Work

You must upload your work once you have some designs and have created an account on a print-on-demand website. Some very popular POD suppliers are:

- ◆ Printify
- ◆ Printful
- ◆ SPOD
- ◆ Teelaunch
- ◆ Teescape
- ◆ CustomCat

Other not so well known POD suppliers are:

- ◆ InterestPrint
- ◆ Gooten
- ◆ Picanova
- ◆ KinCustom
- ◆ Contrado
- ◆ ThisNEW

Many of these POD suppliers have a direct integration with Shopify. They typically provide connection (integration) instructions for your Shopify store.

Promote Your Store

As with any small business, marketing and advertising are a corner-stone for your print-on-demand store. Here are some strategies for marketing your small company:

1. Use sales channels such as Etsy, Walmart Marketplace and eBay. Amazon is not recommended yet as there is so much competition, it is difficult to make a substantial profit.

2. Upload Frequently: Developing the practice of posting frequently will enhance the likelihood that customers will visit your store because there will be more appealing designs and pieces of art. Design and upload something new at least once a week.

Be Patient

Starting to make money with POD might take some time, but that's okay. As long as you put in the work consistently, the money will eventually come.

Tips for Your POD Business

Use Free Marketing Channels to your Advantage

Make sure you've investigated all the available free marketing options before investing any money in advertising. These consist of:

1. Facebook Business Page: More than a third of the world's population uses Facebook each month, making it the most popular social media site online (Mohsin, 2022). Be sure to

name your Facebook business page as close to your Shopify domain as possible.

2. Instagram: With more than a billion active monthly users, this network has overtaken Facebook as the second-largest social media platform (Pew Research, 2017). It's crucial to create a business account on Instagram and connect it with your Facebook business page. Work to get the name of each account as close to your Shopify domain name as possible. This will help build your overall brand image.

3. TikTok: The majority of TikTok users are females between the ages of 10 and 29. Create a branded channel, again naming it as close to your Shopify domain as possible and experiment with content if that is the audience you want to connect with. Follow popular hashtags, join in on the hottest memes, and incorporate them into your brand for your first TikTok sale.

4. Pinterest: Many potential customers use their Pinterest profile to plan their purchase out about 4 months, on average. Create a business profile on Pinterest and, again, make sure you name it as close to your Shopify domain as possible.

5. Twitter: Create a business profile with Twitter and name is, as I've said above, as close to your domain as possible.

Expanding Your Sales

To maintain your momentum after your first sale, first ten sales or more, stick to the following steps:

Evaluate and Assess

Examine the marketing plan that has produced the best results for you. What platforms did you utilize, for instance, and which ones were the most valuable in terms of profit, return on investment (ROI), good feedback, useful relationships, etc.? This will guarantee that you are getting the outcomes you desire.

Assemble Data

You must evaluate the success of your store in light of your past actions to make data-driven decisions. Google Analytics is one of the top tools for data collection. It gives you a comprehensive insight into your company and enables you to improve your marketing strategies.

Establish a Feedback System with your customers

Reviews help you: stand out, establish your reputation, boost search engine rankings, educate your followers about product choices, display customer endorsements on your website, and increase sales. Use review tools to assist you to collect feedback, such as Judge.me, Wiremo, Stamped.io, HelpfulCrowd, Reviews.io, Yotpo, or others.

Finally, be Tenacious in your Marketing Endeavors

If your company isn't expanding as quickly as you had intended, try not to get disappointed. Giving up too soon means squandering chances to learn important lessons for the future. Remain resilient, and have a positive attitude and keep testing, measuring and implementing what works. In addition, stop what is not working.

Final Thoughts and Chapter Summary

In this chapter, you explored the value of high ticket dropshipping and printing on demand and how they can boost your business to new success.

◆ High-ticket items give you more substantial profit margins and broader pricing options.

◆ Print-on-demand services make it simpler to avoid the time, expense, and risk that come with maintaining inventory and enable you to produce customized goods at a portion of the cost of doing it yourself.

◆ High-ticket POD products are items that can give you much higher profit margins than your traditional POD products as there is less competition in the niche.

You can make your website and interaction options perfect and still have your business fail for a completely different reason: poor customer service. In the next chapter, we will go over how poor customer service can hurt your business and what you can do to make your customer service the best possible.

8.

Customer Service

Did you know that a study has found that about 47% of customers discontinue making purchases from a company after receiving subpar customer service? (Salesforce, 2019). This means that you should put a lot of effort into offering top-notch customer service if you don't want to disappoint your customers. Let's go into more detail about this below.

Best Practices for Dropshipping Customer Service

1. Contact us page: This is a straightforward form that mostly collects a customer's email address and requests their questions. You receive a similar email and respond to the sender.

2. Email: An official email would make your customers have confidence in your credibility. In your Shopify admin, you can go to Settings>Domain>Click on your main domain and then enter the primary email addresses you want to have as contacts for your customers, such as sales@domain.com, customerservice@domain.com, yourname@domain.com, returns@domain.com.

Of course, you would insert your actual domain name where I have indicated "domain" in those email addresses. These are some of the basic ones to have. When you set this up in Shopify, it allows you to set a forwarding email address where you will receive those top-level domain emails.

3. Live chat: You don't have to be accessible at all times to use this feature. You can configure the live chat application so that it notifies customers when you will return and automatically responds to their messages.

4. Phone number: Some customers have a mentality that they can only be fulfilled by speaking to someone on the phone. This will significantly raise your reputation. I have gotten most of my numbers from Google Voice (free) or MightyCall.com (small monthly charge).

Tips for Great Customer Service

Pay Attention to What you Hear and Read

Ask questions, engage in dialogue, and deepen your comprehension of your customers. Because they believe you'll be able to better serve them, your customers would like you to understand them.

Clarify Everything you Do

Describe your company's organizational structure and workflow in an honest and open manner. By doing this, you'll establish a positive rapport with customers right away and provide transparency. This is best expanded upon on your About page.

Respond Promptly

Customers anticipate quick response times from customer service. To have a chance at keeping a customer happy, try to respond to their questions within two hours ideally, 24 hours realistically. In a perfect world, you would always have customer support agents available.

Other Techniques for Customer Service

Leveraging a Variety of Communication Channels

Your customers should be able to contact you via live chat, emails, a contact form on your Contact page and phone calls whenever and wherever they need assistance. Long-term, this will improve your relationship with your customers.

Establish a Customer Service Email

Make sure to include a special email address for assisting users with problems. This gives customers the impression that they are speaking with the appropriate person and that their concerns will be handled properly. This can be done within Shopify under the "Domains" section, as mentioned earlier.

Continually Follow Up

This demonstrates to customers that you care about their experience and enhances the reputation of your business. This is also an excellent approach to collect customer feedback on how to enhance your company's operations and product offerings.

Have an FAQ page and a Shipping Policy

Make a page detailing your shipping policies that includes critical details like how orders are handled and sent, as well as the typical wait time customers may anticipate. Shopify includes a template, go to Settings>Policies and you should be able to generate the Shopify policy templates.

Include a FAQ page that addresses the most often asked questions. Customers are more likely to buy from you and be satisfied if they can resolve their own questions on your website.

Add All Product Details on the Website

This is a solid practice for SEO for eCommerce product pages and will aid in preventing problems before they arise. You'll be able to drive more traffic to your product pages and give potential customers sufficient details to make the purchase. It also helps keep down returns and refunds.

Follow-up Strategy

Did you know that 80% of sales are made on the fifth or sixth contact, whereas only one in ten prospects will decide to buy during the initial interaction? (Hayes, 2021)

You're losing out on a chance to increase sales and expand your business if you don't follow up with your present customers or potential customers.

Why a Strong Follow-Up Plan is Essential for your Store

1. It develops trust: It reflects the business's brand look as one that is eager to forge enduring connections.

2. Making an effort to keep your customers engaged will help your dropshipping store differentiate itself from the competition and enforce your brand.

3. It provides customer insights: By keeping in touch with your customers, you can learn important details about their preferences and expectations.

4. It encourages more business by boosting customer loyalty: Companies that follow up with customers on a regular basis are more likely to see repeat business.

5. It increases conversion rates: When you gather customer feedback and address their grievances, eventually they begin to display loyalty for your business.

Common Techniques for Following Up

Welcome Emails

Customers that sign up for your email marketing are really interested in your goods and services. They can become devoted customers with just a brief and easy welcome email from you.

To make the mail more personal, use their first names. This can be automated through an email marketing system such as Mailchimp, or my favorite, Omnisend. You can find Omnisend and other email marketing apps through the Shopify app store.

Periodic Thank-You Notes

Send a customized thank you note to a customer who has just bought anything from your dropshipping company to express your gratitude. You might even give them a gift card or a discount code to use on their subsequent purchase. This can be automated through your review platform. I use the paid version of Judge.me.

Sharing Valuable Resources

Include new customers in your automated onboarding series as soon as they subscribe to your email list. Start sending them a string of instructional and helpful posts and content that responds to their questions and provides answers. Include everything you think they could find interesting. This is usually automated through your email marketing program.

Feedback Collection

Almost all business owners make blunders occasionally. Negative feedback will give you a chance to put your customer's experience right while positive feedback will assist you identify your satisfied customers. Always respond to negative and positive reviews.

Delivery of Reminders

You can prompt your customers to finish their transactions, let them know about future events or new product launches, promote premium products to them, etc. with email reminders and abandoned shopping cart reminders through your automated flows within your email marketing program. Omnisend has a great setup for this.

Up-Selling/Cross-Selling

While you still can display pertinent products on payment pages, you can also include their information in an email that cross-sells or upsells to let your customers know how much money they can save by purchasing a bundle offer rather than a single item or an upgrade.

Loyalty Email

Happy customers are those who return. Marketing experts advise sending a loyalty email 27–28 days after a customer makes a purchase. Any email that you send to your customers qualifies as a loyalty email as long as you're providing value.

Recommending Good Products

You can entice people to go to your website by providing a promotion or coupon that they can use while buying something from your most recent line.

Other Excellent Practices that could Improve the Experience of your Customers

1. The use of open-ended inquiries rather than yes/no questions. The better you understand your customers, the more effectively you can provide them with individualized solutions.

2. Shortening customer wait times. The sooner you get in touch with a customer after a sale, the more likely it is that you may persuade them to make another purchase.

3. Keeping your emails short. Try to write brief, useful material that addresses customers' problems and provides workable solutions rather than lengthy letters.

4. Aiming for a great customer experience in every transaction. Pay close attention to providing an excellent customer experience. Customers will return more frequently if you go above and beyond to keep them satisfied.

Final Thoughts and Chapter Summary

You need to maintain good customer service as a dropshipper since you don't interact with the customers face to face. Here are the important aspects of the chapter.

◆ You should put a lot of effort into offering top-notch customer service if you don't want to disappoint your customers.

◆ You're losing out on a chance to increase sales and expand your business if you don't follow up with your present customers or potential customers using an email marketing app through Shopify.

◆ Pay close attention to providing an excellent customer experience. Customers will return more frequently if you go above and beyond to keep them satisfied.

In the next chapter I give you easy tips on how you can build your brand awareness using several advertising tools.

9.

Building Brand Awareness Through Organic Marketing

With millions of people worldwide being familiar with their logo, I'm sure you'll agree that Coca-Cola is unquestionably the brand with the highest brand awareness. How can you make your target customers this much aware of your brand?

By way of definition, the words "brand awareness" is used to describe how conversant your customers are with your brand, and the solutions you offer. People are conscious of your business and the relevance of your brand to them if they can quickly recall information about it or even associate an emotion with it.

How Important Is Brand Awareness?

Short answer: highly important. The basis of all your marketing initiatives, from media platforms to SEO, must be brand recognition. It's what makes people take notice of your business and the products you have to offer, allowing you to win their trust and influence their purchasing decisions.

Advantages of Brand Awareness

1. Considering that first impressions matter greatly, the more you make people conscious of your brand, the faster you would create a positive perception of your business as well.

2. Building trust requires awareness, and the more people who know about your brand, the more they trust you.

3. It attracts visitors to your website. If your company is the first to come to mind when someone wants to purchase something in your product category, they will visit your website to learn more.

4. It helps people decide who to choose from (you) and why.

The Use of SEO (Search Engine Optimization) in E-Commerce

SEO is the process of improving a website's placement on search engine results pages when a prospective customer types in relevant keywords. It is a great way to raise one's brand awareness and generate revenue without spending money on marketing. This is called "organic" marketing.

SEO for Novices

The use of well-selected keywords is a basic component of SEO. Don't overdo this though, SEO strategies focus on maintaining the balance between several other elements like testimonials, the use of internal and external links, the structure of the site, originality, and the quality of writing. It also removes any flaws that might be stopping your site from ranking higher than other sites in your niche on the Google organic results page.

Key Concepts for SEO Beginners

1. Recommendations for keyword density. The first step in integrating keywords in your web content is to incorporate them in a way that best balances their presence with the total volume of material. Particularly the product listing page.

2. For dropshipping SEO, use H1 tags. Your H1 tag is comparable to a book's title. The product title will be your H1 tag if the page is a product page. It will be the category name if it is a category.

3. Title tags for dropshipping SEO. The title tag is also what appears in the Bookmarks tab when someone bookmarks a specific page or uses the forward and backward browser buttons in the upper left corner of the screen. Make it incredibly simple to use.

4. When you use a search engine, meta descriptions appear immediately after the title tag. This is the first 150 words of your product description. At the bottom of each product

page, you will then find an SEO description that you can update with a short summary of your product description. Use 1-2 primary keywords in the SEO description.

5. Naming your internal links your main keywords is an SEO strategy used to let search engines know which pages you want to appear for particular keywords.

6. In SEO, a sitemap is a list of all the pages on your website that Google should be aware of. You should set up your Google Search Console at https://search.google.com/search-console. This is free of charge and where you would connect your Google Analytics account. This is also where you would submit your sitemap. A sample of the format your primary sitemap would be is https://domain.com/sitemap.xml

Tips & Tactics for SEO

1. Take your original product shots whenever you can to boost your SEO rankings. You can raise your dropshipping SEO ranks by doing this.

2. Add alt tags to your images: Many search engines use these to determine the subject of an image and when to display it to a searcher.

3. Improve the titles of your images by adding captions and titles that are close to or identical to the picture name and alt tag, if you choose to use them. Keep it straightforward and simple to grasp.

4. Craft unique product descriptions; If yours are generic like everyone else's, you run the risk of not being penalized by search engines. So if your products have specifications that are included in a data feed, come up with a creative way to present or discuss the specifications rather than just copying and pasting the data.

What Not To Do

1. Search engines don't accept forum comments and links since they are so simple to create and anyone can obtain them.

2. Automated link builders are computer programs that post comments on blogs, forums, and communities on your behalf using bots and spiders. This approach may result in negative brand perception among bloggers and relevant internet groups.

3. Creating link farms is another method for websites and services to be mapped and punished.

4. Sponsored posts: You should probably collaborate with legitimate influencers, but make sure everything is "no follow" so that your site doesn't put itself at further risk of being penalized.

Email Marketing

Sending advertising messages to present and potential customers via email to sell, inform, or cultivate loyalty is known as email marketing.

In eCommerce, this is used to send transactional, promotional, and lifecycle messages, and so is a particularly crucial marketing technique.

Why Email Marketing is Essential for Success

1. The periodic emails help you maintain a relationship with your customers.

2. This marketing strategy is extraordinarily effective at generating sales not just from a first visitor, but also from your returning customers.

3. This marketing strategy can directly impact the 3 key growth factors for your brand. It can win back efforts and boost a customer's number of sales, your conversion rates can be raised by using scheduled welcome and discarded cart emails, and lifecycle ads can seamlessly target the right customer demographic with high-value goods.

4. Email marketing is unaffected by outside gatekeepers or third parties and as such, your marketing strategies won't be derailed by any unforeseen changes to algorithms.

Steps to Set Up Your Email Marketing Campaign

Begin by choosing the email marketing program you'll use to organize your list. A few platforms that work well with Shopify are Klaviyo and Omnisend. Then, compile your email lists. Your subscribers must decide to join your mailing list though, for this to happen. You can get them on board by following these steps:

Create a page before you launch

Create a straightforward page before you formally open shop and ask your site visitors to subscribe to your email list to stay in the loop. Write material that highlights the exciting aspects of your new product and includes compelling rewards for early subscribers (such as 10% off on the day you launch).

Compile the emails of your subscribers and initial customers
After a customer places their first order, provide them the choice to register an account. With Shopify, you can invite customers to activate their accounts directly.

Insert your subscription forms on different pages on your website
Your header, footer, About Us page, and blog page are some good places to try inserting your subscription forms. You can use tools like Omnisend, Mailchimp, Privy, Sumo, or JustUno from the Shopify App Store to curate these pop-up notifications.

Use lead magnets to speed up signups
Run contests, provide special offers, and provide as many informational materials as possible to get more customers to subscribe to your mailing list.

Do not infringe on your subscribers' rights.
Your relationship with your mailing list must be founded on permission; this is important from both a marketing and legal perspective. Use double opt-in when creating your email marketing campaigns.

Types of Email Marketing Campaigns

Transactional Emails

These are more practical and convey important information to specific customers during checkout and other purchasing actions. Emails confirming the shipment of an order, receipts, feedback emails, and order confirmations all fall under this heading.

To Improve Your Order Confirmation Emails:

1. Recommend add-ons to give your customers the option to purchase an improved version of the products they are interested in. (A smart way to upsell, isn't it?)

2. Offer a limited-time discount code or free shipping for a future purchase.

3. Politely ask the customer to subscribe to your mailing list by highlighting the values of such membership.

To Improve Your Shipping Confirmation Emails:

1. Make tracking orders simple for your customers.

2. Encourage the buyer to recommend the products they bought to their friends by sending a link to the item on your website.

3. Include detailed product recommendations along with a buyer's purchase.

To Improve Your Customer Feedback Emails:

1. Focus more on the overall satisfaction of your customers rather than simply making sales.

2. After a customer submits any feedback, send them a personalized mail to thank them for their helpful feedback, and for shopping your site.

3. Include customer reviews as user-generated material on the product page to attract more traffic to your site. Judge.me works well for this.

Promotional Emails

These are marketing emails aimed at increasing public knowledge of a certain offer or promotion. Examples of promotional emails are Black Friday sales emails, a Mother's Day gift recommendation email, a summer savings newsletter, or a limited-time-only discount email.

To Improve Your Promotional Emails:

1. Create limited-time promos that relate to the interests of your customers.

2. Offer special deals to your subscribers periodically.

3. Keep your subscribers as informed as possible about forthcoming sales and festivities such as; Father's Day, International Women's Day, after-Christmas and spring clearance sales, etc.

Lifecycle Emails

This last category of email campaigns derives its name from the fact that it is often delivered in response to a customer's specific behavior in the course of the period of such a person being a customer. For instance, a cart abandonment email doesn't go out until the buyer discards their cart, a welcome email is only sent when someone opts to join the mailing list, etc.

To Improve Your Cart Abandonment Reminders:

1. Craft your reminders in fun or exciting ways.

2. Offer an incentive to encourage your customers to complete their orders; eg., a free ebook or a coupon code.

3. Make a clear and specific call to action.

To Improve Your Welcome Emails:

1. Provide as much value as possible to your new subscribers from the start.

2. Send off your welcome emails to new subscribers as soon as possible. This can be automated through Omnisend or Klaviyo.

3. Clarify the frequency of your emails from the start so that subscribers wouldn't feel overwhelmed down the line.

Foundational Metrics for Your Email Marketing Campaigns

List Expansion and Size
The more potential customers you can reach to increase sales, the bigger your mailing list should be. Use your email service provider to see how many new subscribers you've added on a weekly, monthly, or between your most recent broadcast email basis to keep track of this number.

Click-Through and Open Rates
The percentage of emails that were opened by subscribers in an email campaign is known as the open rate. The percentage of emails in a campaign that received at least one click is known as the click-through rate. With both metrics, you can figure out how effective your emails are to spot the changes that need to be made. For instance, if many people opened an email but only a few of them clicked the call to action, you might want to draft a better call to action (CTA).

Deliverability Rates
Your deliverability rates will suffer for all subscribers if you are frequently flagged as a spam sender. This could happen when you focus excessively on selling a product, use large graphics and illegible text, or if you send emails to outdated customers you haven't reached out to over a long period.

Conduct A/B Split Tests
To conduct an A/B test, group your sample recipients into groups A, B, and C. Send two different campaigns to the first two groups to figure out which of the messages was received better than the other. The

winning version, whether it be A or B, will then be sent to your final group of recipients (C). By first testing certain messaging, design, and calls to action with a smaller proportion of subscribers, A/B testing enables you to identify and reliably send high-performing emails.

Revenue

This metric asks the question: how much of your company's overall sales can be attributable to email marketing? The answer to this would direct your decision-making to optimize your campaigns better.

Lifecycle Automation

This metric is rooted in the acronym 'RFM' and is essentially a database marketing phrase that might assist you in categorizing your customer. RFM is an acronym for recent, frequent, and monetary.

1. The recency is the period since a customer made their most recent purchase. (R)

2. The entire number of purchases made by a subscription or customer is their frequency. (F)

3. The total amount spent by a customer—the total of all of their orders—is their monetary value. (M)

You can identify and characterize practically any step in the customer lifecycle using these three metrics.

10.

Building Brand Awareness Through Paid Marketing

When you consider paying for advertising, the first thought that most business owners have is to get Google Ads started. Businesses can use the Google Ads platform to generate ads that advertise their goods in Google search results and on websites that are part of the Google AdSense network. It's a great way to set bids, monitor sales performance, and handle marketing issues as they arise.

Guidelines For Google Ads Optimization

1.   Google Ads and Google Shopping Ads are two slightly different approaches. Google Ads will allow you to set up a campaign without needing approval. However, Google Shopping Ads needs to go through the Merchant Center and you send your product feed automatically from Shopify to Merchant Center through the Symprosis app. This part of Google requires you get approved.

2. Google Shopping Ads uses your product listing as your advertisement, so it's important to have keywords in the titles and descriptions of all of your products.

3. With Google Ads, you can select which keywords to improve the visibility of your ads by creating appropriate product-targeted ad groups. This also lets you track the performance for every category separately.

4. Use appropriate keywords for your audience and items to make sure that customers who are searching for your specific products notice them.

5. Write catchy headlines and test out different ads to decide on the version which could have the greatest positive impact on your campaign.

6. Publicize promos, discounts, and special offers to attract more customers to your store.

7. Use eye-catching pictures or videos to make the most of each view on your advertisement.

8. Use seasonal phrases to your advantage to attract potential customers.

9. Test a variety of ads to determine the most effective one. Choose the language that succinctly outlines the advantages of your items to increase click throughs and help you reach your sales targets.

10. Optimize your bids smartly so that you can decide where to allocate more resources from your budget.

11. You may modify your Google advertisements as you go along to better meet the needs of your business, so don't worry about every tiny detail.

12. Use negative keywords with caution. Negative keywords can help you filter traffic from Google but only when used properly.

13. It's okay to make a few mistakes along the way. Continue to experiment with new things, improve what is already working, and discard what is not.

Kinds of Google Ad Campaigns

1. Google Shopping campaigns: These are popular because, with them, you can easily advertise your products at the top of the Search Engine Results Page on Google.

2. Search campaigns: This campaign centers on spreading awareness of your brand and your items, which will ultimately increase traffic to your website.

3. Product advertising campaigns: With the use of this campaign, you would attract interested customers to your items by advertising your deals through email marketing campaigns, social networking sites, mobile websites, and apps.

4. Competitor search campaigns: These are utilized to monitor your competitor's strongest keywords. You can increase the visibility of your adverts by using the same keywords as your rivals.

5. Remarketing campaigns: By showing ads to people who recently visited your site or used particular keywords in their search queries, remarketing allows you to stay at the top of your audience's minds.

Setting Up Your Google Account

1. To begin using Google advertisements on Merchant Center, register for a Google Merchant account on the Google Merchant Center.

2. Connect your merchant account to a Google shopping feed in your Shopify app. Store. The one I use most frequently is Symprosis Google Shopping Feed. Symprosis has several apps for Shopify.

3. It could take some time to get your products approved through Google Merchant Center, so be patient. You have to be approved through Merchant Center in order to have your Google shopping ads account approved.

4. Make sure to use keywords in your product descriptions and titles.

5. Prepare your test campaigns once your products are certified.

Benefits of Using Google Ads

1. It makes it possible for you to connect with potential customers and for them to learn about your items.

2. It's a great way to increase brand recognition and drive traffic.

3. You can easily and effectively set up campaigns to assess what is best suited for your store.

4. Using the Google Ads platform for advertising requires no special equipment. All you need is time, some money, and avid imagination.

5. You can easily target your customers based on their geography, gender, passions, and past behavior. In a nutshell, you can customize your advertisements to draw in the right kind of people.

6. By monitoring the effectiveness of your adverts, you can adjust them as necessary to get better results.

7. By using remarketing campaigns, you can reach customers who have already been to your business or expressed interest in your merchandise.

Google Shopping Ads: What Are They?

Simply said, Google Shopping Ads are product ads that show up on Google when you search for a specific phrase. These advertisements are great because they display direct product listings on a website featuring the item's image, price, and merchant name in addition to customer reviews.

Advantages of Utilizing Google Shopping

1. Superb Returns On Investment (ROI): Shopping Ads are very successful and have a high click-through rate since they provide all the necessary information to potential customers.

2. Reach a huge audience: Each day, Google handles more than 3.5 billion queries. These advertisements can be seen not only in search results but also on partner websites like Google Images and Google Display Network.

3. Amazing product visibility: To make your goods more visible and to help you draw in more customers, Google Shopping advertisements offer all the details about your product.

4. You only need to set up a product feed in Google Merchant Centre for it to be simple to set up and manage. Everything else will be handled automatically. Remember, the Symprosis Shopping Feed is the one I use on all my sites and recommend.

5. Useful performance tracker: By comparing your campaigns' clicks, impressions, conversion rates, and other metrics, you

can quickly identify what is working and what isn't. This is available through the Google Ads dashboard.

Procedure For Setting Up

1. To get started, get to the 'Register' page on Google Ads and select "Start Now" to open a Google Ads account. Supply your details as accurately as possible.

2. Follow the prompts to register a Google Merchant Center account. Click on "Get Started."

3. Configure your merchant account to meet your needs. This includes creating a return and shipping policy, adding sales tax, and other related things. You need to make sure you have your website in order with contact information and all the legal pages within Shopify. Ensure your refund and return policy is very clear.

Guidelines for Improving Google Shopping Ads

1. Improve product feeds: Your advertisement's product information and image should be of the highest caliber.

2. Separate your campaign structure to make it simpler for you to determine which product is the most well-liked and warrants a larger investment.

3. Locate the winning products: Log into your Google Ads account and select "Shopping" in the left column to find the

winning products. Next, seek items with the highest conversion rates and highest click through rates (CTR).

4. Get rid of the losers; regardless of how much you appreciate a product, if it isn't bringing in any revenue within six months, it is a waste of time.

5. Use negative keywords: Non-converting traffic is unproductive and will just cost you money. Negative keywords are frequently used to restrict the searches and clicks and focus on more productive traffic.

6. Adjust your bid: place a higher bid where your product has a better chance of succeeding. This is done through the Google Ads dashboard in the left column menu under "Show More" at the bottom and then "Schedule." Set up a schedule first that tracks periods of six to eight hours at a time. Then, revisit this section after four to six weeks. You will see what conversions and clicks happen at certain times of day. Reduce your weekday bid and raise it on the weekends if you determine that the weekends are a better time to sell.

7. Avoid making significant adjustments if your advertisement is going successfully. The Google algorithm can get complicated and unpredictable.

Retargeting Customers

Simply put, retargeting is a means of reminding those visitors who left your page without placing any orders of your unique offerings in a bid to get them back. Retargeting campaigns often involve re-engaging with your audience, boosting your sales, and fostering customer loyalty.

When Are Retargeting Campaigns Appropriate?
Retargeting is intended to be a long-term marketing tactic for businesses with an established customer base. Aside from this though, retargeting campaigns are best used in any of the instances below:

Promoting blockbusters
This is especially helpful because promoting goods that your current customers adore (and have rated highly) can help turn your new visitors into buyers and boost the return on investment for your advertising.

Presenting new products
This way, anywhere your site visitors go online, your retargeting advertising will attract their attention, luring them back to your store to see what's new.

Increasing brand recognition
This is important because most prospective customers need to feel like they know you before they decide to buy your goods or service.

Remarketing Efforts Versus Retargeting

The terms "retargeting" and "remarketing" are similar in that they both aim to accomplish the same ends. They both target groups that have either already been to your website or are somewhat familiar with your brand. Both campaigns can also help you build a long-lasting relationship with your target customers through increased sensitization and brand awareness campaigns.

Despite these similarities, however, both marketing efforts often rely on different strategies for achieving their end goals. For instance, on the one hand, retargeting typically uses sponsored ads to focus on potential customers who have already visited an eCommerce website or business page on social media. On the other hand, email marketing is the main tool used in remarketing campaigns to reach out to customers who have already used one's brand. Google remarketing advertising is also used more in remarketing (as opposed to retargeting) to help entrepreneurs turn their site visitors into loyal customers.

How Retargeting Works

The way retargeting works is that after visiting your website, a visitor will begin to see your advertising while browsing other websites, reading articles, listening to music, or shopping online. When they're ready to make a purchase, your advertising will bring them back to your website by reminding them of all the awesome things you have to offer.

How To Retarget The Appropriate Demographic

I would strongly advise you to begin your retargeting efforts with a categorization of your target customers or site visitors. Not only would this help you figure out the reasons why they aren't placing orders on your site, but it would also help you understand their preferences so that you can curate ads personalized to them. You can categorize your customers under the following categories:

Cart abandoners
Since these shoppers were just one tap away from completing their transaction when they simply got distracted for a variety of reasons, retargeting would likely be the most useful tactic for them.

1st-time users
Since they just discovered your page, you can tell that something caught the attention of the customers in this segment in the first place. All you have to figure out is what that attraction is.

Returning customers
These people are not merely visitors to your page. They have bought products from your brand in the past. Since you already have a relationship with them, all you'd have to do here is remind them that you still exist and that you have several items that could be great for their needs.

Recent visitors
These are potential customers who have visited your site in the past without completing their purchases. Now that they are visiting again, your retargeting efforts will make them place that first order and perhaps return to your site on some other day.

How To Time Your Retargeting Campaigns
Generally speaking, the kind of demographic you're targeting and the kind of product you're offering will determine exactly when to commence your retargeting campaign. The best times to retarget are:

Immediately when a customer leaves your site

When a customer leaves your site, retarget them with the product that is still in their cart on your site. This will serve as a gentle reminder for them to return and finish their purchase.

During special or festive seasons

Holidays and special events are excellent times to retarget your customers because such seasons allow business owners to communicate with their customers more subtly (eg., through newsletters, discount offerings, greetings emails, and so on). You can pique your would-be customers' interest at such times with information on a new product line, improved service, or some discount on the items still sitting in their carts.

Before your products go bad

If you notice that a product your customer purchased with a shelf life is going to expire, you can give them the opportunity to reorder by using retargeting ads based on their previous purchases. This can apply to expiring food items (fresh or preserved), cosmetic products, subscriptions, and everything else in between.

Intermittently

Don't bother a customer with the exact ad again after they've placed their orders. In such instances, you can either try to upsell or cross-sell to them. (More on these later).

How To Use The Proper Message While Retargeting

When you've decided on the categories of customers you'll be retargeting, take into account these five suggestions to put together the ideal message for them:

Your choice of designs

Make sure that your brand logo appears prominently on your retargeted advertisement so that your viewers can easily recognize it. Keep your choice of designs simple but eye-catching with a specific call-to-action that is thoughtfully positioned.

The language used

It's best to use an active (as opposed to a passive) verb in your call to action. Also, use the least amount of words (a short sentence or two) possible to pass your message across. Ensure that the language emphasizes the advantages of the products, not merely their qualities.

Use appropriate displays

Target your recent site visitors and cart abandoners with the products they left in their carts, your 1st-time visitors with special promotions like free deliveries, and your returning customers with either an upsell or cross-sell product that goes well with their latest purchase or serves as a reminder to them to replace an item that is soon to expire.

Remember your target demographics

Retarget your customers based on their interests so you can make a more tailored offer and increase the likelihood they will return to your site and complete their orders.

Google Analytics

E-Commerce is a cutthroat industry, and it can be challenging for some business owners to gauge the profitability of their operations. With

Google Analytics, you can access data on your store and do a more accurate analysis of its performance over time.

How Can Google Analytics Benefit Your Drop Shipping Business?

Since it gives you the opportunity to gather and evaluate detailed information on your customers' demographics, areas of interest, and interactions with your store, Google Analytics is a highly relevant tool in the dropshipping business model. You can use this information to make data-driven decisions on how to best enhance your site.

How to Set Up a Google Analytics Ecommerce Report

Begin by activating 'eCommerce reports' on Shopify and Google Analytics. Next, navigate to your profile on Google Analytics. Choose "Admin," and then pick the type of view that suits your website. Go to "Ecommerce Settings" and click 'enable' after choosing the view that best suits your online store. Turn on your eCommerce reports, you should have access to data from your online store easily using the following.

Understanding your demographics

The demographics of your customers, particularly the behavior of males and females in your store, is a crucial metric that you can examine. By choosing the "Acquisition" tab in your Google Analytics sidebar, followed by the "Demographics" and "Male/Female" options, you can obtain this data.

Understanding the behavior of customers

You could also be interested in the "Behavior" section under the "Acquisition" tab because it will provide you with more insight into your customers. Additionally, it gives you a thorough insight into how brand-new and recurring visitors engage with your brand and its offerings.

Purchasing habits

This section gives you information about various areas of your store that you can improve. Choose "Conversions" from the menu on the left-hand side of your Google Analytics and then "E-commerce," to access this data.

Transaction effectiveness

This shows you the number of people who visited your business within a specific period and actually bought something from you. This may be accessed by clicking the "Conversions" tab on Google Analytics' left side, followed by the "E-commerce" and "Transactions" tabs.

Checkout performance

You would learn more about customer behavior throughout the check-out process at your store by using this section. Click on "Conversions" on the left side, followed by "Ecommerce" and "Checkout," to get this information.

Product functionality

The products you sell in your eCommerce store will be included in this section of Google Analytics, and you'll be able to highlight the best-performing ones. Here, you can check helpful metrics like page visits, sessions, average time on page, and conversions. This part of Google Analytics can be accessed by clicking on "Conversions," then choosing "E-commerce," and then choosing "Product."

In general, you can benefit from its features, especially the crucial indicators, to notably enhance your dropshipping business.

Joining Relevant Communities

The process of marketing your business is dynamic. Picking up tips from fellow dropshippers is a great way to expand your understanding and vision for your brand. And the easiest way to do it is by joining the online communities in your niche.

Advantages of Participating in Online Communities

1. Free Advice and Knowledge: Just by listening to and reading conversations, you can learn a lot.

2. Introduction to New Ideas: Participating in online forums with a wealth of current and pertinent discussions can introduce you to subjects you had never heard of before.

3. You meet and interact with interesting people who would often challenge you with their different ways of reasoning and resolving complex issues.

4. Obtain Honest Feedback: Sincere community members will point out your mistakes and suggest ways to strengthen your performance.

5. Gain Industry Knowledge: If you join a restricted community that vets its members, this advantage is very potent.

6. Acquire Leads and Conversions: As community members come to rely on you as an authority, they will come to you for your goods and services.

7. In the end, it's a terrific method to meet others who have similar interests.

Where to Look for the Ideal Marketing Communities

1. Facebook: One of the finest places to uncover marketing groups that suit your needs is Facebook. By going to the Groups section of your Profile page and looking up your subject, you may browse free groups. I don't recommend paid Facebook ads, yet. You lose too much money learning it.

2. Forums: Since they are often privately held, these are excellent resources for learning about marketing. For instance, a forum dedicated to graphic design might devise a more effective method of displaying pictures that participants upload along with their posts.

3. LinkedIn: Even though LinkedIn is frequently used to identify marketing networks, it is not nearly as widespread compared to the other platforms. Still, based on your needs, you can discover some useful groups here.

How to Maximize the Benefits of Online Communities

1. Adhere strictly to the community rules, especially if you're a new member.

2. Refrain from requesting assistance from others. Ask instead about DIY options or resources for further information. This will make you respected in the community.

3. Stay on topic in discussions or you could be banned for submitting off-topic material.

4. Always give more than you receive. People will eventually start to value you as a member and will be eager to assist you should the need arise.

5. Never be hesitant to switch the subject to email or another platform if you meet someone fascinating in a group.

6. Follow the trend to remain informed. You will learn a lot more about your business model.

7. Finally, encourage conversations, even when they don't benefit you directly. This will strengthen your value as a member over time.

Final Thoughts and Chapter Summary

To bring this book to a close, you can see how building a brand acts as a last step that encompasses all of the above-mentioned business-boosting aspects. This chapter covered quite a bit of content, so let us look at some of the more important points here in summary.

◆ Brand awareness is what makes people take notice of your business and the products you have to offer, allowing you to win their trust and influence their purchasing decisions to grow your brand.

◆ SEO is the process of improving a website's placement on search engine results pages when a prospective customer types in relevant keywords.

◆ With Google Ads, you can select which keywords to improve the visibility of your ads by creating appropriate product-targeted ad groups. This also lets you track the performance for every category separately.

◆ Google Shopping ads are advertisements that display direct product listings on a website featuring the item's image, price, and merchant name in addition to customer reviews.

◆ With Google Analytics, you can access data on your store and do a more accurate analysis of its performance over time.

Final Words

The dropshipping business model is an incredibly profitable one. Its challenges are not always easy to navigate but I have learned that the key is to be forgiving of yourself and to not give up. Remain open and teachable through every step of your journey. Your profits will come and overall, you'll be a better entrepreneur for all your challenges.

I hope this book has inspired you to get your business back on track. I hope you learned a thing or two about kickstarting your brand, beginning today.

We will conclude this journey by highlighting the things we learned throughout this book:

◆ In Chapter One: We learned all about the dropshipping e-commerce landscape today, including its current statistics and popular trends.

◆ In Chapter Two: We discussed all the reasons why your Shopify store may not be earning enough revenue. We also highlighted the key factors you should consider before relaunching your brand along with the Dos and Don'ts of dropshipping business.

◆ In Chapter Three: We focused on the importance of operating within a niche. We also learned all about niche strategies and listed some of the most profitable niches in the dropshipping industry.

◆ In Chapter Four: We extensively discussed how to find credible and reliable suppliers for your dropshipping business.

◆ In Chapter Five: We discussed the process of re-launching your Shopify store by choosing a good Shopify theme and redesigning the website.

◆ In Chapter Six: We covered the importance of reviews, how to analyze competitors, upselling, and cross-marketing as some features a successful Shopify store must have.

◆ In Chapter Seven: We learned about high-ticket dropshipping and print-on-demand.

◆ In Chapter Eight: We discussed the importance of providing great customer service to improve our relationship with our customers and increase sales.

◆ In Chapter Nine: We rounded up our discussion by covering the importance of building brand awareness and highlighting how to maintain and grow a Shopify dropshipping business, with topics concentrated on the marketing aspect.

Thank you for coming on this journey with me. If this book has helped you in any way, please share your honest reviews on Amazon. I'd love to hear from you.

With all my heart, I wish you the best of luck in all that you do.

Sources

Ask Attest. (2021, June 11). The Importance of Brand Awareness

   https://www.askattest.com/blog/articles/the-importance-of-brand-awareness

Bloem, Craig. (2017, July 31). 84 Percent of People Trust Online Reviews As Much As Friends. Here's How to Manage What They See.

   https://www.inc.com/craig-bloem/84-percent-of-people-trust-online-reviews-as-much-.html

Business Wire. (2020, October 9). Dropshipping Market Forecast to 2027 - Global COVID-19 Impact and Analysis by Product Type, Organization Size, and Geography

   https://www.businesswire.com/news/home/20201009005175/en/Dropshipping-Market-Forecast-to-2027---Global-COVID-19-Impact-and-Analysis-by-Product-Type-Organization-Size-and-Geography---ResearchAndMarkets.com

Charlton, Graham. (2012, March 20). Ecommerce customer Reviews: Why You Need Them And How To Use Them.

   https://econsultancy.com/ecommerce-customer-reviews-why-you-need-them-and-how-to-use-them/#i.35yv7v2okfp7yq

Coyne, Jon. (2021, September 2). 5 Key Things To Consider When Relaunching Your Ecommerce Website.

   https://www.venditan.com/blog/5-key-things-to-consider-when-re-launching-your-ecommerce-website

Dennis. (2020, March 30). Level Up Your Online Marketing by Joining Communities

https://wpsimplepay.com/level-up-your-online-marketing-by-joining-communities/

Dolan, Laura. (2020, March 7). How To Retarget Customers

https://keap.com/business-success-blog/sales/sales-process/how-to-retarget-customers

Dopson, Elise. (2022, April 22). Is Dropshipping Worth It in 2022? 6 Things To Know.

https://www.shopify.com/blog/is-dropshipping-worth-it

Draper, Alan. (2022, September 15). 5 Ways to Enhance Customer Experience in E-commerce

https://www.business2community.com/ecommerce/5-ways-to-enhance-customer-experience-in-e-commerce-02264218

ERP Information. (2022, July 12). Dropshipping Trends 2022 And Future Predictions.

https://www.erp-information.com/dropshipping-trends#New_dropshipping_trends_to_look_out_for_in_2022

Fenner, Trevor. (2022, September 22). High Ticket Dropshipping: Finding Profitable Products and Suppliers

https://www.ecommerceceo.com/high-ticket-dropshipping/

Ferreira, Corey. (2021, January 1). How to Find and Work With Reliable Dropshipping Suppliers.

https://www.shopify.com/ph/blog/dropshipping-suppliers

Ferreira, Corey. (2022, April 4). The 13 Best Dropshipping Suppliers in 2022.

https://www.shopify.com/blog/dropshipping-suppliers

Forrester Research. (2012, June 21). Consumers Drive Channel Preference To Achieve Effortless Customer Service

https://www.forrester.com/blogs/12-06-20-consumers_drive_channel_preference_to_achieve_effortless_customer_service/

Grand View Research. (2022). Print On Demand Market Size, Share & Trends Analysis Report By Platform (Software, Service), By Software (Stand-alone, Integrated), By Product (Apparel, Home DÃ©cor, Drinkware), By Region, And Segment Forecasts, 2022 - 2030.

https://www.grandviewresearch.com/industry-analysis/
print-on-demand-market-report

Global News Wire. (2020, October 6). Global $591 Billion Dropshipping Market Forecast to 2027

https://www.globenewswire.com/news-release/2020/10/06/2104052/0/en/Global-591-Billion-Dropshipping-Market-Forecast-to-2027.html

Hayes, Ricky. (2021, February 5). Dropshipping Business: Eight Effective Follow-Up Strategies For Your Dropshipping Business

https://debutify.com/blog/dropshipping-business-eight-effective-follow-up-strategies-for-your-dropshipping-business/

Hooked Design and Marketing. (2020, February 10). The Importance of Website Traffic.

https://hookedmarketing.net/blog/the-importance-of-website-traffic/

Howard, Molly. (2022, May 3). How To Start a Print-On-Demand Business As a Designer

https://www.gcu.edu/blog/performing-arts-digital-arts/how-start-print-demand-business-designer

Intribe. (2021, July 15). What Is Cross-Marketing? How It Works and Examples.

https://www.intribe.co/blog/what-is-cross-marketing

Jaumann, Jenny. (2021, February 21). 10 Steps To Find Out If Your Niche Ideas Are Profitable.

https://affcoups.com/blog/find-out-if-your-niche-ideas-are-profitable/

Kabbage American Express. (n.d). Dropshipping: Do's and Don'ts

https://www.kabbage.com/resource-center/manage/the-dos-and-dont-of-drop-shipping/

Kraftly University. (n.d). 7 Ways To Spot Fake Dropshipping Wholesalers.

http://university.kraftly.com/shipping-fulfillment/7-ways-spot-fake-dropshipping-wholesalers/

Kraftly University. (n.d). 7 Ways To Spot Fake Dropshipping Wholesalers

http://university.kraftly.com/shipping-fulfillment/7-ways-spot-fake-dropshipping-wholesalers/

Kotula, Yurii. (2021, September 21). 15 Must-Have Ecommerce Features For Websites.

https://intelvision.pro/
blog/15-must-have-ecommerce-features-for-website/?nowprocket=1

Kumar, Braveen. (2021, June 1). Print on Demand: A Low-Risk Way to Sell (2022 Playbook)

https://www.shopify.com/blog/print-on-demand

Macdonald, Mark. (2020, March 11). Learn Email Marketing: Everything from List Building to Advanced Lifecycle Automation

https://www.shopify.com/ph/blog/email-marketing

Mailchimp. (n.d). What Is Retargeting?

https://mailchimp.com/en-gb/resources/what-is-retargeting/

Malamut, Caroline. (2016, May 25). 14 Compelling Customer Reviews Stats You Need to Know in 2016.

https://blog.capterra.com/customer-reviews-stats-you-need-to-know/

Meola, Andrew. (2016, March 30). Returning Customers Are Far More Valuable To Online Retailers Than New Customers.

https://www.businessinsider.com/e-commerce-report-shows-returning-customers-are-more-valuable-than-new-ones-2016-3?r=US&IR=T

Mohsin, Maryam. (2022, June 15). 10 Facebook Statistics Every Marketer Should Know In 2022.

https://www.oberlo.com/blog/facebook-statistics#:~:text=Facebook%20has%20
2.80%20billion%20monthly,site%20on%20a%20daily%20basis.

Nexcess, Maddy. (2021, June 25). Top 7 Ecommerce Website Features: What Customers Want in an Ecommerce Site.

https://www.nexcess.net/blog/what-customers-want-in-an-ecommerce-site/

Nguyen, Lavender. (2021, April 20). The Ultimate Guide to Starting a Print-on-Demand Business [Updated 2022]

https://printbest.com/blog/
the-ultimate-guide-to-starting-a-print-on-demand-business-in-2021/

Niche Dropshipping. (n.d). Customer Service For Dropshipping: The Ultimate Guide.

https://nichedropshipping.com/customer-service-for-dropshipping/

Oberlo. (n.d). What Is Upselling?

https://www.oberlo.com/ecommerce-wiki/upselling

Patel, Sujan. (2016, November 21). 10 Reasons Your Ecommerce Store Isn't Making Any Sales.

https://www.entrepreneur.com/article/283888

Pew Research Center. (2017, January 11). How often Americans are using social media.

https://www.pewresearch.org/internet/chart/
how-often-americans-are-using-social-media/

Podium. (n.d). 5 Powerful Advantages of Google Reviews.

https://www.podium.com/article/advantages-of-google-reviews/

Reimer, Adam. (2018, December 30). The Beginner's Guide To Dropshipping SEO.

https://www.oberlo.com/blog/guide-to-seo-101

Repriser. (2020, February 12). Dropshipping Suppliers: How To Find The Best Ones.

https://www.repricer.com/blog/dropshipping-suppliers/

Riach, Andrew. (2017, May 23). Use Google Analytics for Your Ecommerce Business

https://www.oberlo.com.ph/blog/google-analytics-ecommerce-business

Rozkalne, Karlina. (n.d). How to Make Your First Sale With Print-on-Demand

https://www.printful.com/uk/blog/
how-to-make-your-first-sale-with-print-on-demand

Saleh, Khalid. (2022, May 16). The Importance of Online Customer Reviews.

https://www.invespcro.com/blog/
the-importance-of-online-customer-reviews-infographic/

Salesforce. (n.d). What Is Upselling?

https://www.salesforce.com/eu/learning-centre/sales/upselling/

Salesforce. (2019, May 1). 40 Customer Service Statistics To Move Your Business Forward

https://www.salesforce.com/blog/customer-service-stats/

Sattar, Kamil. (2021, July 22). 10 Profitable Dropshipping Niches In 2021.

https://www.forbes.com/sites/forbesbusinesscoun cil/2021/07/22/10-profitable-dropshipping-niches-in-2021/?sh=37452c415bd8

Sam, Chris. (2022, October 15). Google Shopping Ads for Dropshipping Product Promotion

https://dropshippinghelps.com/ how-to-promote-dropshipping-products-in-google-shopping-ads1/

Schooley, Skye. (2022, September 16). How To Find Your Business Niche.

https://www.businessnewsdaily.com/6748-business-niche-characteristics.html

SendPulse. (n.d). What Is Cross-Marketing? The Basics

https://sendpulse.com/support/glossary/cross-marketing

Sprout For Business. (n.d). 6 Common Website Problems.

https://sproutforbusiness.com/blog/post/increasing-website-leads

Shogun. (2022, February 7). The Ultimate Checklist for Relaunching Your Ecommerce Website

https://getshogun.com/enterprise/relaunching-your-ecommerce-website

Shopify Staff. (2022, September 1). What Is Upselling? Upselling Definition With Examples.

https://www.shopify.com/blog/what-is-upselling

Tasmia, S. (2022, March 7). Google Ads for Dropshipping: In 2022, what must you know?

https://dropshiplaunchpad.com/google-ads-for-dropshipping/

Truitt, Leigh-Anne. (2020, June 9). The Inside Scoop on Ecommerce Reviews: Why They Matter and How to Make the Most of Them

https://www.bigcommerce.com/blog/online-reviews/

Tyrrell, Paige. (n.d). 15 Common Online Shopping Problems Causing Revenue Loss for Your Business (+ How To Fix or Avoid Them).

https://www.prefixbox.com/blog/online-shopping-problems/

Made in United States
North Haven, CT
21 October 2023

43014868R00104